War and revolution in Vietnam, 1930–75

introductions to history

Series Editor: David Birmingham,
Professor of Modern History, University of Kent at Canterbury

A series initiated by members of the School of History at the
University of Kent at Canterbury

War and revolution in Vietnam, 1930–75

Kevin Ruane
Canterbury Christ Church College

UCL PRESS
UCL
PRESS
Taylor & Francis Group

First published in 1998 by UCL Press

UCL Press Limited
1 Gunpowder Square
London EC4A 3DE
UK

and

1900 Frost Road, Suite 101
Bristol
Pennsylvania 19007-1598
USA

The name of University College London (UCL) is a registered
trade mark used by UCL Press with the consent of the owner.

British Library Cataloguing-in-Publication Data
A catalogue record for this book is available from the British Library.

Library of Congress Cataloging-in-Publication Data are available

ISBN: 1-85728-323-6

Typeset in Sabon and Gill Sans
by Acorn Bookwork, Salisbury, UK.
Printed and bound by T.J. International, Padstow, UK.

Contents

Preface

This book is an introduction to one of the most bloody, protracted and controversial conflicts of the twentieth century. As such, it aims to provide the reader with a basic chronological account of events in and to do with Vietnam from 1930, when the Vietnamese Communist Party was founded, through to 1975 and the final triumph of the Vietnamese revolution. It also seeks to offer a simultaneous on-going discussion of the way in which historians have interpreted the conflict.

Two themes in particular dominate the narrative: war and revolution. With regard to the former, in recent years historians have started to write of the Vietnam *wars*, in the plural, as opposed to the Vietnam *war*, in the singular, an approach that strongly informs the present study. Vietnam in the twentieth century has been the scene of a colonial war of reconquest and, conversely, a war of colonial resistance and national liberation; it has been the centre of a Cold War confrontation-by-proxy between the United States and the major communist powers, the Soviet Union and Communist China; and it has witnessed a civil war between the Vietnamese themselves. These are just three variations on the theme. Admittedly, it is sometimes hard to say where one war ended and another started, but the term Vietnam 'war' is neither an appropriate nor adequate description of what took place. The second major theme is revolution. From the very outset in 1930, the Vietnamese communists committed themselves to two revolutionary goals: national liberation for Vietnam and, thereafter, the construction of a socialist and ultimately communist state. A continuing examination of how these aims were adhered to over almost half a century, how the communists resisted hugely powerful counter-revolutionary forces (most notably the United States), and the reasons behind their ultimate victory in 1975 provides a further thematic thread to the narrative.

One of the dangers confronting the writer of a short introductory text on Vietnam is that the temptation to deal with *all* that happened will lead to an end-product that is both cursory and superficial, to an annotated chronology of events rather than a critical examination. Having perceived this danger very early on, I chose to sacrifice breadth of coverage for some depth of analysis. Some readers will therefore be disappointed to find Laos and Cambodia relegated to the periphery of the discussion when there are many historians who quite rightly regard both countries as central players in the Vietnamese drama, not the bit players I have cast them as. Likewise, my limited treatment of the American anti-war movement, as well as my generalized approach to military strategy and tactics, will doubtless dismay others. In defending my selective approach, I can do little more than hide behind a cliché: a study of this kind cannot cover everything. My hope instead is that what I do cover, I cover well, and that the work is recognized as merely a platform for further investigation of Vietnam.

I would like to express my gratitude to a number of people who, in various ways, have helped me during the writing of this book. Professor Sean Greenwood and Dr James Ellison, both of Canterbury Christ Church College, read large sections of the manuscript and offered pertinent and valuable comments; Mr R. A. Burrows drew on his own first-hand experience of the conflict in Vietnam in commenting upon *several* drafts of the book, and I owe him particular thanks for the care and attention he brought to the task; Professor David Birmingham of the University of Kent, the Series Editor, and Steven Gerrard and Aisling Ryan of UCL Press, must have wondered how such a short book could take so long to write, but for their patient understanding I thank them, too; Penny Evans, one of my research students at Canterbury Christchurch College, found herself in the unusual position of being able to criticize the work of her supervisor – and did so, though always constructively; my 'America in Vietnam' course groups of 1995–6 and 1996–7 were the testing ground for many of the ideas in the book; from those two groups, Christopher Underwood deserves to be singled out for the enthusiasm he brought to the role of sounding-board; the Research Committee of Christ Church College for financial assistance; and lastly, my especial thanks to Catherine Donaldson, to whom this book is dedicated.

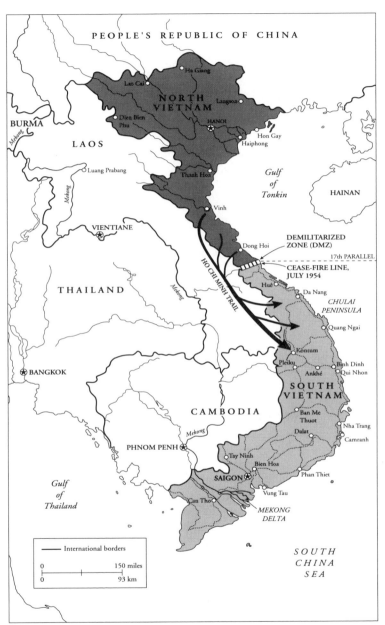

Vietnam after 1954

CHAPTER ONE

The making and unmaking of a revolution, 1930–46

In February 1930, a small group of Vietnamese communists met together in Hong Kong. Political exiles from their own country where they were wanted by the French colonial authorities, the gathering took place – legend has it – at a football match. By the time the final whistle blew, a single and united Vietnamese Communist Party had been formed. Presiding over the conference was Ho Chi Minh, a well-known nationalist and communist.[1] Ho and his comrades committed themselves to the creation of an independent and communist Vietnam, hence to two revolutions, a national and a social. In pursuit of these goals, they would eventually humble a European colonial power and bring to its knees the world's first superpower.

It is impossible to separate the early fortunes of Vietnamese communism and nationalism in the twentieth century from the career of Ho Chi Minh. Ho was born in 1890, just three years after French imperial expansion in Southeast Asia had climaxed in the establishment of the Union of Indochina. In conquering Vietnam, the French had divided the country into three administrative sectors, roughly commensurate with its traditional-historical regional composition. The three *kys* of Vietnam – Tonkin (the north), Annam (the centre) and Cochinchina (the south) – were combined with Laos and Cambodia to form French Indochina. It was in Annam, in Nghe An province, that Ho Chi Minh was brought up. Encouraged by the patriotic fervour of his father and affected by the injustices of colonialism that

---

[1]Ho Chi Minh ('He who Enlightens') was the best known of the many pseudonyms adopted by the man born Nguyen Sinh Cung.

he witnessed on a daily basis, by late adolescence he had evidently developed a rudimentary nationalist consciousness. In 1911, then aged twenty-one, Ho secured a menial job on a French liner operating out of Saigon. What prompted his decision to leave Vietnam is unclear. Indeed, as one of his biographers has pointed out, due to the paucity of reliable documentary evidence, the story of much of Ho's life is 'fragmentary, open to dispute, a mere approximation of the truth' (Lacouture 1968, 4). There is, nevertheless, little doubt that his subsequent travels were crucial to his political development and proved, in retrospect, to be the making of Ho the nationalist, the communist and the revolutionary. After several years at sea, in 1917 Ho arrived in France. There, however, he encountered not the superior civilization depicted in colonial propaganda, but a country buckling under the strain of the First World War – a country from which Vietnam's independence might yet be wrested.

Ho quickly established himself as the chief spokesman for the expatriate-Vietnamese nationalist community in Paris and, in this capacity, he petitioned the great powers gathered at the 1919 Versailles peace conference in the hope of securing their support for the principle of freedom for all colonial peoples. When this démarche achieved nothing, a disappointed Ho looked elsewhere for inspiration and soon found it in the success of the Russian Revolution which, in 1917, had shown that a ruling élite, no matter how powerful and entrenched, could be overthrown. Ho went on to join the French Socialist Party and, when the Party split in December 1920 on the question of affiliation to the Third Communist International (Comintern), he sided with the radical minority that broke away to form the French Communist Party and accept direction from Moscow. Ho's decision was influenced by the Socialist Party's lack of interest in colonial issues and, more positively, by the political philosophy of the Russian leader, Lenin. In his celebrated *Theses on the National and Colonial Question*, published in 1920, Lenin had urged communists in colonial areas to join with peasants and patriotic elements within the urban middle class to confront and destroy their imperialist masters, whereupon the communists could dispense with their moderate allies and assume power in their own right. In Marxism-Leninism, therefore, Ho found both a means of realizing his nationalist objectives and an attractive blueprint for Vietnam's post-colonial future (Ho Chi Minh 1973, 250–2).

By 1923, Ho had emerged as the French Communist Party's leading voice on colonial matters. In fact, so effective was he in this role, that he was invited by Comintern to study Marxist ideology at its head-quarters in the Soviet Union, a singular honour. Ho arrived in Moscow in January 1924 at the moment of Lenin's death, an event that saddened and troubled him. 'In his lifetime he was our father, teacher, comrade, and adviser', Ho wrote in a tribute in *Pravda*. But Ho also questioned, on behalf of colonial peoples everywhere, whether Lenin's successors would likewise 'spare their time and efforts in concerning themselves with our liberation' (Fall 1967, 39–40). Ho was right to be worried. Whereas Lenin had acknowledged the revo-lutionary potential of the peasantry and had advocated worker–peasant alliances in backward countries, the new Kremlin leadership lionized the industrial proletariat as the only vehicle of revolution. Ho, representing a predominantly peasant constituency in Vietnam, strongly disputed this view at the Fifth Comintern Congress in 1924 but was, he later recalled, a 'voice crying in the wilderness' (Duiker 1995, 27).

Towards the end of 1924, Ho was sent by Comintern to Guangzhou (Canton) in southern China at a point when the dominant Chinese nationalist movement, the Guomindang, was in alliance with both the Soviet Union and the Chinese Communist Party. Aware that neither Comintern nor the French communists viewed Vietnamese emancipa-tion as a priority, Ho took the opportunity to organize the younger and most zealous elements in the large expatriate Vietnamese com-munity in Guangzhou into an embryonic revolutionary organization. Anti-colonial discontent was widespread in Vietnam, whether amongst the peasantry, which made up almost 90 per cent of the population, the small industrial working class or the urban educated, professional and commercial strata of society. But when, on occasion, this discontent had converted itself into open protest, it had been localized, uncoordinated and easily suppressed by the French. To Ho, the way to realize the latent revolutionary potential of the Vietnamese was to create a small but highly-motivated organization that could unite and then lead the masses in pursuit of self-determination and an egalitarian society. Such, indeed, were the aims of the Vietnamese Revolutionary Youth League, the fruit of Ho's labours in China. The League, however, was something less than a fully fledged Communist Party, and Ho accepted that its members would require extensive ideological and revolutionary induction before that appellation could be justified. Initial training occurred at a self-styled 'institute' in

Guangzhou itself, with the most promising recruits despatched to Moscow to complete their education at the Stalin School for the Toilers of the East. By the late 1920s, it is estimated that the League had over 1,000 activists inside Vietnam, promoting its revolutionary-nationalist programme and recruiting new members. This, however, was as far as the League got. The accession of the bitterly anti-communist Chiang Kai-shek to the Guomindang leadership in 1927 brought with it an abrupt and bloody end to the *modus vivendi* with the Chinese communists. In the ensuing chaos, the League disbanded in an act of self-preservation and Ho escaped back to Moscow. By 1929, its residual leadership had succumbed to factionalism, one wing maintaining that national liberation had to take precedence over all else, another – dominated by Comintern-trained ideologues – insisting on the primacy of class struggle and an end to recruitment from all sources other than the small Vietnamese industrial proletariat. There is little question that Ho Chi Minh's sympathies lay with the nationalist faction.

At the start of 1930, Comintern, keen to heal this rift, ordered the Hong Kong 'unity' conference referred to earlier. However, the unity that emerged involved more concessions to the Comintern faction than the nationalists, with the formation of a Vietnamese Communist Party perhaps the biggest concession of all. Whilst Moscow quickly gave the new Party its seal of approval, Ho, from a nationalist standpoint, must have had doubts about the wisdom of the decision. National independence – Ho's first goal if not Comintern's – undoubtedly required the active involvement of the widest possible range of anti-French opinion in Vietnam, but a revolutionary movement that espoused overtly communist objectives for the post-liberation period risked alienating the very non-communists needed to make the national revolution in the first place. On 18 February 1930, following the appointment of a provisional Central Committee to reside inside Vietnam, the new Party issued a manifesto in which, for the moment at least, national and social goals were in rough equilibrium. It comprised ten points:

1) To overthrow French imperialism, feudalism, and the reactionary Vietnamese capitalist class.
2) To make Indochina completely independent.
3) To establish a worker–peasant and soldier government.
4) To confiscate the banks and other enterprises belonging to the

imperialists and put them under the control of the worker–peasant and soldier government.

5) To confiscate the whole of the plantations and property belonging to the imperialists and the Vietnamese reactionary capitalist class and distribute them to poor peasants.

6) To implement the eight-hour working day.

7) To abolish public loans and poll tax. To waive unjust taxes hitting the poor people.

8) To bring back all freedoms to the masses.

9) To carry out universal education.

10) To implement equality between man and woman.

(Fall 1967, 129–30)

By the autumn of 1930, however, a combination of Comintern injunctions and the alacrity with which the dominant Moscow faction in the Central Committee acted upon them, resulted in the reworking of the Party programme to conform more closely to the preferences of the Soviet Union. In 1928, Comintern had called upon its members in colonial areas to 'bolshevize' both their organizations and revolutionary aims. However, in its initial desire to give equal prominence to national and social objectives, and to promote a broad-based alliance of workers, peasants and progressive bourgeois elements in pursuit of its aims, the Party had fallen out of step with Comintern. Therefore, in October 1930, the Vietnamese communists voted to relegate national liberation to a position of secondary importance, to prioritize the social revolution, and to acknowledge the industrial working class as the engine of that revolution. The Party's name was also altered from the Vietnamese to the Indochinese Communist Party (**ICP**), presumably to encourage co-ordinated action throughout the region, although the Vietnamese communists were to remain the backbone of the Party.

For Ho, these changes must have been hard to accept. In under a year, his nationalist agenda and his pragmatic 'united front' strategy had become marginalized within the Party he had done so much to create. Historians have devoted considerable time and attention to the question of Ho's priorities. Was he a communist first and foremost? Or did his nationalist aims predominate? The answer, it seems, is that he was both in equal measure; he wanted Vietnam to be free *and* communist. On the other hand, so great was Ho's patriotic fervour, that many writers now agree that he was not fighting to liberate Vietnam from the French (and, later, from the Americans and their

Vietnamese proxies) simply to deliver it up to another external power, whether it was the Soviet Union or, after 1949, Communist China. In that sense, Ho was less of an *international* communist than his early Moscow connections might suggest. As his troubled relationship with Comintern in the 1930s shows, he was much more an *independent* nationalist–communist.

The early 1930s were lean years for the ICP, years of survival rather than advancement of the revolutionary cause: 1931 was especially bleak, with brutal French retaliation following communist involvement in major peasant revolts in central Vietnam. According to communist sources, the embryonic Party apparatus was decimated, with 2,000 members killed and over 50,000 supporters arrested. Up to 90 per cent of the Party's Vietnam-based leadership were imprisoned or executed (Duiker 1996, 41–2). Ho Chi Minh, however, witnessed these events at a distance: arrested in Hong Kong by the British, he was later released and, in 1933, returned to Moscow. Those Party cadres that survived the French repression stayed on in Vietnam and set about building a permanent base in the northwest of the country, in the mountainous area known as the Viet Bac. Inaccessibility to the French was the initial attraction of a mountain redoubt, but in time the decision came to acquire greater significance as it ensured that communism was more deeply rooted in northern Vietnam than in the south.

The Comintern faction continued to dominate ICP decision-making throughout the 1930s and, as such, the industrial proletariat rather than the peasantry remained the principal target of Party propaganda and recruitment. To others in the Party – to that section identified with the absent Ho Chi Minh – this approach constituted a wanton disregard for the revolutionary potential of the rural masses. In the summer of 1935, however, Comintern suddenly announced a dramatic shift in its world outlook, calling on communists everywhere to promote 'popular fronts' in an effort to counter the growing menace of fascism. All anti-fascists were to be considered potential allies, regardless of class complexion, as Moscow, unnerved by the threat from Nazi Germany, put the defence of the Soviet Union before all other considerations, even ideological consistency. In many ways, Moscow's new line resembled Ho Chi Minh's preferred method of dealing with the problem of French rule in Vietnam. As a consequence, the pragmatic-nationalist wing of the ICP began to reassert itself at the expense of the doctrinaire graduates of the Stalin School. But Ho would have been less happy with Moscow's insistence on a policy of neutrality towards the French: communists in Vietnam were free to participate in a broad-based anti-fascist coalition, but were forbidden from using it to undermine French rule. From the Soviet standpoint, this made good sense, as communist-led anti-colonial activity would run counter to its European objective of a collective security agreement with France (and Britain) against Germany. But to Ho, this must have been further proof that Comintern was merely an arm of Soviet foreign policy, and that the promotion of international revolution – and more particularly the Vietnamese revolution – was of little concern to the Kremlin.

None the less, the ICP endorsed the new approach out of respect for international communist discipline, and in May 1936 received a quick reward when a Popular Front government in France granted the ICP semi-legal status and released large numbers of political prisoners from Vietnamese jails. The Party made the most of its freedom, openly organizing and recruiting amongst urban workers and the peasantry. But the respite from repression was short-lived. The collapse of the French Popular Front in 1938 brought a clawing back of concessions by its right-wing successor, a process that gathered pace following the outbreak of the Second World War in Europe in September 1939. Thereafter, with the Soviet Union in effective alliance with France's traditional enemy, Germany, the colonial security forces in Vietnam turned on the ICP with a vengeance. Faced with the threat of extinction, elements of the Central Committee issued a call for a general uprising leading to national liberation. In the event, the move from political to armed struggle was hopelessly premature, and French suppression of poorly organized insurrections in Tonkin and Cochinchina in 1939 and 1940 was fierce and effective, especially in the south. It appears to have been the Comintern-trained members who bore the brunt of the French onslaught, for they were never to be a force again. Significantly, their demise ensured that those who would go on to rebuild and lead the Party would be advocates, like Ho, of the creative adaptation of Comintern injunctions to suit the social, economic and political conditions peculiar to Vietnam and, by extension, the particular needs of the Vietnamese revolution (Kahin 1986, 10).

In June 1940, the war in Europe had an even more far-reaching impact on the Vietnamese situation when France capitulated to Germany and the umbilical cord linking it to its overseas empire was severed. In Vietnam, an isolated French administration was powerless to resist occupation by an expansionist Japan. From the summer of 1941 onwards, the French ran Indochina on behalf of the Japanese who, in turn, derived considerable military-strategic advantages from its geographical position. The wider war that engulfed Asia and the Pacific following the Japanese attack on Pearl Harbor in December 1941 initially made little difference to the Vietnamese, most of whom continued to labour under what Ho Chi Minh called a 'double yoke' of imperialism (Gettleman 1995, 4). Yet, difficult as the years of Japanese occupation were, to Ho and other ICP leaders viewing the situation from southern China, they were not without their compensations. Working on the premise that Japan would eventually be defeated, a moment of opportunity (*thoi co*) would present itself – the chance to fill the ensuing power vacuum before the French re-filled it. But success in this endeavour would require intensive preparation.

With this consideration in mind, Ho secretly entered Vietnam in February 1941, the first time he had set foot in his country for thirty years. His travels, and then his Comintern commitments and the effectiveness of French colonial security had contributed to his lengthy exile, but in May 1941 Ho presided over the ICP Central Committee's Eighth Plenum, held at Pac Bo in Tonkin. By the close of this momentous meeting, agreement had been reached on the construction of a Vietnamese Independence League (*Viet Nam Doc Lap Dong Minh*) *Hoi*, otherwise known as the Vietminh. Although the Vietminh was to be organized and directed by the ICP, Ho and his colleagues determined to do so with a hidden hand. The appeal of Marxism-Leninism was never going to be sufficient to establish the kind of mass organization needed to defeat the French and the Japanese. An appeal to the deep-seated nationalism of the Vietnamese people, on the other hand, had far greater potential, especially in tandem with a commitment to economic justice and social welfare for all. The intention, in short, was to create a patriotic-nationalist umbrella organization, but with the handle of the umbrella held firmly in concealed communist hands. Come *thoi co* (the Allied defeat of Japan), the Vietminh would seize power in the name of the Vietnamese people. Then, after the national revolution had been consolidated, the ICP would gradually assert itself within the Vietminh and proceed with the execution of its political and social agenda.

For Ho, a further reason for obscuring the ICP's control of the Vietminh was the hope of winning international support for Vietnamese independence. In particular, the American government, by its very public championing of the principle of self-determination for all peoples, encouraged nationalists in colonial areas to believe that, come the end of the war, they would have powerful support for their cause. Had Ho and the Vietminh been aware of it, they would have drawn even more encouragement from President Franklin D. Roosevelt's strong personal interest in the fate of Indochina in general and of Vietnam in particular – an interest derived from firm anti-colonial convictions, a perception of French rule as especially harsh, a contempt for the meekness of the French capitulation to Germany in 1940, and a detestation of Vichy France's subsequent collaboration, not just with Germany in Europe but with Japan in Southeast Asia. The result was a determination, oft and simply stated during the war, that 'French Indochina must not be turned back to the French' (LaFeber 1975, 1285). Instead, Roosevelt wanted the territories placed under a paternalistic 'trustee', answerable to the nascent United Nations, that would guide them to full independence over a period of twenty or thirty years. Yet, for all his enthusiasm, Roosevelt's plan never came to fruition.

One reason was the President's choice of trustee. Geographical proximity and political orientation suggested the Guomindang, but Roosevelt's belief that China would emerge from the war united under Chiang Kai-shek and able to assume international responsibilities was a serious delusion, confirmed in the spring of 1944 when nationalist–communist tensions, in abeyance since the Japanese invasion, resurfaced and a resumption of civil war threatened. British opposition was another impediment. The Churchill government was alarmed lest a precedent be established whereby all colonies – including British territory in Asia then occupied by Japan – would be given over to the United Nations. In consequence, London's criticism of the trusteeship concept was unrelenting. But perhaps the strongest argument against the scheme arose in the context of the growing Anglo–American confrontation with the Soviet Union in 1944–5 over the future of Eastern Europe. With the Grand Alliance increasingly unlikely to outlive the war that spawned it, many in Washington, if not yet the President himself, considered it foolhardy to alienate the French over Indochina when they might soon be needed to help contain the spread of Soviet power in Europe.

On 8 April 1945, in agreeing that trusteeships should operate on a voluntary basis only, Roosevelt acknowledged the defeat of his hopes, for it was obvious that the post-liberation French government of

General Charles de Gaulle had no intention of giving up Indochina. The death of the scheme therefore pre-dated its author by four days (Roosevelt died on 12 April), a chronological juxtaposition that gives the lie to the argument of some historians that if Roosevelt had lived the French would never have returned to Vietnam and the course of history, be it French, Vietnamese or American, would have changed for the better. By the same token, it is clear that Roosevelt's successor, Truman, did not, as sometimes attested, destroy the scheme. With the Red Army's occupation of Eastern Europe seen as a possible precursor to a Soviet play for power throughout the Continent, Truman and his advisers made the promotion of stable and friendly governments in Western Europe a top priority. To this end, they moved to eliminate sources of US–French friction, a process that included support for a French restoration in Indochina. This was the first occasion, but not the last, on which America's Vietnam policy was constructed in relation to European imperatives. The new direction of US policy was confirmed at the last Big Three conference of the war, at Potsdam in July 1945, when agreement was reached that the Japanese surrender in Vietnam (whenever it came) should be overseen by Nationalist China in the north and by British forces in the south, the 16th parallel being the dividing line. In supporting this military expedient, the Truman administration cannot have been ignorant of its political ramifications – it guaranteed the return of the French to southern and quite probably northern Vietnam. As for the moment of that return, this appeared to be brought closer when, following the atomic bombing of Hiroshima and Nagasaki in August, Japan surrendered and the Second World War in Asia and the Pacific ended. However, developments within Vietnam over the preceding four years had ensured that the restoration of French colonial rule would be strongly resisted by the combined forces of native nationalism and communism.

In June 1941, shortly after the founding of the Vietminh, Ho Chi Minh had issued an appeal to the Vietnamese people that provides an insight into the breadth of constituency he hoped to capture. Ho called on 'Elders! Prominent personalities! Intellectuals! ... Rich people, soldiers, workers, peasants, employees, traders, youth and women who warmly love your country!' He went on to emphasize patriotic themes at the expense of communist sloganizing, although in his peroration he gave a hint that his ideological goals had not been lost sight of. 'Let us rise up quickly! Unite with each other, unify your action to overthrow the Japanese and the French', he urged. 'Victory to Viet-

Nam's Revolution! Victory to the World's Revolution!' (Fall 1967, 134). Thereafter, alongside the critical tasks of recruitment, organization and propaganda, the Vietminh evolved a politico-military strategy for effecting its goals. On the political level, a reform programme was developed for areas liberated from the French and Japanese that encompassed land redistribution, rent reductions, labour protection, the substitution of a single progressive tax for the pernicious Franco–Japanese impositions, and a literacy campaign. Special attention was paid to the peasantry, for success hinged on mobilizing the rural masses and maximizing their revolutionary potential. In this connection, the promise of land and justice had a strong allure. On the military front, Vo Nguyen Giap, a former history teacher, an ICP member since the 1930s and a student of Mao Zedong's guerrilla war philosophy, undertook the creation of a Vietminh army to be trained and based in the Viet Bac, although arms were in very short supply. Locally based armed units were also established, linked by a nationwide network of communication, to harass the Japanese and the French in the short term. Come *thoi co*, regular and irregular Vietminh forces would combine in a military offensive which, if the political groundwork had been successful, would have widespread popular support.

Meanwhile, in mid-1941, Ho returned to China in search of military assistance for the Vietminh, only to be arrested and imprisoned by the Guomindang. Although he managed to procure his release in 1943 he none the less failed in his main objective of securing arms from Chinese sources. Ho was similarly unsuccessful in attempts to recruit powerful Western allies. Encouraged by Washington's high profile anti-colonialism, he made a number of direct appeals to Roosevelt to recognize his movement as the legitimate representative of the Vietnamese people, all of which went unanswered. But contacts in 1945 between the Vietminh and the China-based American OSS (Office of Strategic Services), the forerunner of the CIA, proved more encouraging. The OSS came to rely on the Vietminh for intelligence on Japanese troop movements and the location of downed US pilots in Indochina and, in exchange, provided Ho with precious arms, ammunition and communications equipment. The relationship grew closer when American agents actually arrived in Vietnam in May 1945, making direct contact with the Vietminh. Anti-colonial in outlook, unconcerned by the Vietminh's communist hue and ignorant of the shifts in policy towards Vietnam occurring in Washington at the time, the OSS probably encouraged Ho to expect official US support come the end of the war as a reward for his assistance during it.

The last months of the Second World War saw events inside Vietnam begin to move in favour of the Vietminh. On 9 March 1945, the Japanese, possibly anticipating an Allied invasion and concerned that the French would act as a fifth-column, interned French colonial officials and military personnel and assumed full control of the country. Vietnam was granted its 'independence' under the former emperor of Annam, Bao Dai, who established a native puppet government. For the Vietminh, the March 'coup' provided unprecedented freedom to prepare for its own assumption of power, as Japanese authority – in the absence of French back-up – was limited to Cochinchina and the larger urban areas of Annam and Tonkin. By June 1945, the Vietminh's writ ran large in ten northern provinces, enabling Ho to designate them a 'liberated zone' and implement social, political and economic reforms. Meanwhile, on the military side, Giap merged his small Viet Bac-based élite force with local units throughout the country in a new national Vietnamese Liberation Army.

Having worked on the assumption that power would be seized province-by-province in the wake of liberating Allied forces, the Vietminh were initially wrong-footed by the Japanese surrender on 15 August 1945. A new approach was quickly devised, however, that emphasized the importance of establishing a functioning nation-wide administration in advance of the arrival of the victorious Allied powers who, when faced with evidence of the ability of the Vietnamese to run their own affairs, would hopefully accept the country's *de facto* independence. Accordingly, on 16 August, the Vietminh leadership issued a call for an immediate insurrection and then set up a Vietnam National Liberation Committee to orchestrate affairs. Over the next two weeks, Giap's Liberation Army (now around 5,000 strong, but with perhaps 50,000 irregulars in support) seized control of towns and villages throughout Tonkin and Annam, riding on a wave of popular enthusiasm and meeting little armed opposition. On 18 August, the Japanese puppet government was ousted and, shortly after, Bao Dai abdicated. By the end of the month, though its sway was less than total in Cochinchina where rival nationalist groups were active, the Vietminh could, with justification, claim to be *the* political power in Vietnam; impeccable patriotic credentials, a truly national organization, and a proven capacity to mobilize popular support underscored this claim (Duiker 1995, 52). On 2 September, Ho Chi Minh stood before a crowd of half a million in Ba Dinh square in Hanoi and declared his country independent.

With this, the founding of the Democratic Republic of Vietnam (**DRV**), the Vietnamese revolution appeared complete. Yet, within less than two weeks, it had started to unravel. On 13 September, in accordance with the Potsdam agreement, around 1,500 British–Indian troops arrived in Saigon under the command of Major General Douglas Gracey with orders to accept the Japanese surrender and repatriate prisoners-of-war but otherwise refrain from entanglement in local politics. But Gracey, personally committed to assisting French restoration, had few qualms about exceeding his authority. On 23 September, he ordered the release of nearly 2,000 French troops, interned since the March coup, and turned a blind eye as they proceeded to oust the Vietminh from power. Faced with a violent Vietminh backlash, Gracey augmented his forces with some 5,000 recently disarmed Japanese troops, dragooned under threat of trial as war criminals. The combined efforts of British, French and Japanese units eventually secured control of Saigon and its environs. The British Labour government never disavowed Gracey's actions and, in October 1945, recognized the French civil administration as the sole authority in Cochinchina. A huge influx of French troops followed, many transported to Vietnam in American ships. By the time the British mission ended in March 1946, French military strength totalled around 65,000 men. During this period, Vietminh forces waged a desperate rearguard action, but it was unavailing in the face of superior firepower. Appeals by Ho Chi Minh for American support went unanswered by a Truman administration more than ever determined to do nothing to jeopardize the support of France in the emerging Cold War in Europe.

In northern Vietnam, meanwhile, 180,000 Guomindang troops had arrived to take the Japanese surrender and, in the process, asset-strip the area. The beleaguered Vietminh took steps to placate the Chinese. In November 1945, for example, the ICP dissolved itself, a concession to the anti-communist Guomindang, although in practice communist domination of the Vietminh continued at a clandestine level. And following elections to a National Assembly in January 1946, a number of DRV government positions were given to pro-Guomindang representatives. Such measures ensured that, unlike the British in the south, the Chinese did not set out to destroy Vietminh authority, only circumvent it – an important distinction as it held out the possibility of a resumption of Vietminh power in the future. That was, if the Guomindang resisted the temptation to fashion the northern provinces into a vassal state in line with traditional Chinese regional goals. Indeed, so concerned was the Vietminh leadership by this danger that its overriding priority became the removal of the Chinese. But how was this to be achieved, given the Vietminh's military weakness? Reluctantly, Ho came to see a negotiated French return as the only solution to the dilemma. Explaining his thinking to bewildered followers who, only a few months earlier, had been celebrating their country's independence from France, Ho emphasized that it was only a tactical retreat:

> Don't you realize what it means if the Chinese stay? Don't you remember your history? The last time the Chinese came, they stayed one thousand years. The French are foreigners. They are weak. Colonialism is dying out. Nothing will be able to withstand world pressure for independence. They may stay for a while, but they will have to go because the white man is finished in Asia. But if the Chinese stay now, they will never leave. As for me, I prefer to smell French shit for five years, rather than Chinese shit for the rest of my life.

> (*Pentagon Papers* 1971, I, 51)

Talks between Ho and Jean Sainteny, French commissioner to Vietnam, began in late 1945 and produced an agreement on 6 March 1946. Under its terms, France acknowledged the DRV as a free state *within* the French Union (a federation of metropolitan France and its overseas territories). This meant that whilst the DRV would exercise autonomy over most internal affairs, France would retain control of foreign, defence and commercial policy. Ho consented to the presence of 15,000 French troops in the north, to replace the Chinese, on the understanding that they would be withdrawn over the following five years. Lastly, and crucially from the DRV standpoint, there was to be a referendum in Cochinchina to determine whether or not it should unite with the rest of the country – whether, that was, the Democratic Republic of Vietnam would comprise the whole of Vietnam. Ho and Sainteny agreed to further negotiations, this time at governmental level, to explore ways in which this limited independence could be extended in the future. Meanwhile, a cease-fire would bring an end to the fighting in the south, raging since 23 September 1945.

Where did the balance of advantage lie? It is difficult to see any winner other than the French. Without firing a shot they had obtained military re-entry into the north, whilst the price – their political concessions – was hardly binding. Ho, on the other hand, recognizing the weakness of the Vietminh's bargaining position, had little choice other than to rely on French good faith. Even so, it is likely that confidence in Ho's leadership of the Vietminh (if not the subterranean Communist Party) was damaged by his association with an arrangement that, coming so soon after defeat in the south, seemed to give up the last of the gains of the August revolution.

French forces moved north immediately, entering Hanoi on 18 March 1946. Within a few weeks their numbers had reached, and probably exceeded, the agreed total of 15,000. The Vietminh meanwhile strengthened its hold on the DRV by ejecting from the government those pro-Guomindang members installed during the Chinese occupation. In Cochinchina, the French colonial regime did little to prepare for the planned referendum, fuelling the doubts of many in the Vietminh about the entire March agreement. Indeed, as insurance against the day when independence might have to be fought for, the Vietminh continued to develop its armed forces. At the base of what might be described as a military pyramid stood village militias, units of five or six volunteers on permanent standby to assist the operations of the regionals who occupied the central section. The regionals were also volunteers but organized on a provincial rather than village basis to support the regular or standing army that stood at the apex of the pyramid. The latter was trained and maintained in two base areas, the Viet Bac and a newer one to the south of the Red River delta in Tonkin. As of early 1946, however, the Vietminh forces remained poorly armed and no real match for their French counterparts.

Despite these military precautions, the Vietminh leadership must have been encouraged when the French consented to formal political talks in Paris in June to build on the Ho–Sainteny accords. But all such optimism evaporated when the Vietminh delegation arrived in France to learn that during their journey, the French High Commissioner in Indochina, Admiral Thierry d'Argenlieu, had declared Cochinchina an 'autonomous republic'. D'Argenlieu, a diehard colonialist who had condemned the March agreement as a new 'Munich', had acted unilaterally. But the refusal of the French government to issue a disclaimer indicated official support for a separate Cochinchina. It is difficult to exaggerate the importance that Ho and his colleagues attached to a fully-integrated Vietnam and, by extension, their dismay at d'Argenlieu's actions. As one historian has observed, as communists, 'they *might* have accepted a smaller but communist state that could conceivably have been free of the French [but] it was as nationalists that the Vietminh argued their case for indissoluble national unity' (Short 1986, 50).

The DRV delegation might well have returned home straight away were it not for the possibility of reversing d'Argenlieu's action in direct negotiations with the French government. However, for five weeks there was no government to negotiate with, as the Fourth Republic lurched from one political crisis to the next. Eventually, a new centre-right coalition was formed under Georges Bidault, but in the ensuing conference at Fontainebleau the French demonstrated that they had no intention of repudiating the annexation of Cochinchina, still less of granting full independence to any part of Indochina. Nearly all French politicians believed that the restoration of their country's tarnished *grandeur* was inextricably linked to the preservation of the French Union. Vietnam was seen as the key to the cohesion of the Union as a whole, for any concession to the Vietminh might inspire nationalist rebellions in more important colonial areas like Algeria. Thus the DRV delegation left France at the end of August 1946 with nothing to show for their efforts. Ho, however, stayed on in the hope that personal diplomacy might yet avert disaster in Vietnam. Within the Vietminh, evidence points to the existence of a growing 'war party', ready to use the breakdown of the diplomatic process as an excuse to launch what Ho feared would be a premature and possibly doomed war of liberation. 'Don't let me go back empty-handed', he allegedly implored the Minister for Overseas France, 'arm me against my own extremists' (Lacouture 1968, 124). What Ho eventually took back was the so-called *modus vivendi* of 14 September 1946 by which the French, in return for certain economic concessions in northern Vietnam, promised not to victimize Vietminh supporters in Cochinchina, and hinted (no more) that a plebiscite might yet materialize in the south. A further round of talks was scheduled for the spring of 1947 and, in the interim, both sides agreed to renounce violence as a method of settling their differences.

Unfortunately, the *modus vivendi* did little to arrest the drift to war in Vietnam. In Saigon, the colonial authorities, fearing that another swing of the political pendulum in Paris could produce a government ready to compromise with the Vietminh, began to consider offsetting this danger through pre-emptive military action. This said, there was by this stage as much chance of the opening shot being fired by the Vietminh. Ho, on his return from Paris, had been hard pressed to sell the *modus vivendi* to his followers, many of whom were deeply suspicious of French intentions and saw full independence arriving only through armed struggle. By the autumn of 1946, war was thus only a flashpoint away. It eventually came on 20 November, when French troops seized a vessel in the port of Haiphong thought to contain arms bound for the Vietminh. The local DRV administration claimed the French had overstepped their jurisdiction, a skirmish ensued and shots were exchanged. General Etienne Valluy, the commander of French forces in Indochina, seized on the incident to 'teach the Vietnamese a lesson', a remark that has also been attributed to Bidault and d'Argenlieu, from which one may infer considerable French support for the sentiment (Young 1991, 30; Kahin 1986, 23; Buttinger 1973, 89). On 23 November, after the Vietminh had failed to respond to an ultimatum requiring them to withdraw completely from Haiphong, Valluy ordered a naval bombardment of the Vietnamese quarter of the city. Vietminh forces tried to hold the position but, by 28 November, the whole of Haiphong was under French control. Loss of life on the Vietnamese side was considerable – a figure of 6,000, mostly civilians, is commonly cited. Whether Valluy acted independently or on orders from higher political authority has never been fully resolved, but the fact that the French government never condemned the action is instructive.

In the aftermath of Haiphong, many in the Vietminh favoured an immediate call to arms. Yet Ho chose to keep open channels of communication with the French and to try and resist the clamour for war. Though his endeavours were destined to come to naught, one wonders why he persisted at all. Two possible answers offer themselves. The first is that Ho wanted to delay the moment of ultimate confrontation to strengthen the Vietminh's military position and, by extension, its prospects of success. The second is consistent with Ho's obvious preference for a non-military solution: if a semblance of peace could be maintained, in time a new government might emerge in Paris, leftist in orientation and prepared to take the Vietminh seriously. But time was something that the forces of French colonialism, bullish and confident after Haiphong, were not prepared to give him. On 19 December 1946, attention shifted to Hanoi, the DRV's capital. When the commander of the French garrison in the city ordered the Vietminh to lay down their arms, Giap, acting on instructions from the Vietminh leadership, declared the start of a war of nation-wide resistance. The following day, even Ho accepted the inevitable and issued a personal appeal to 'the entire people to wage the resistance war' (Fall 1967, 162). Rioting erupted throughout Hanoi, but the French were well prepared and responded with full force, eventually driving the Vietminh from the city. So began the first Vietnam war, though in truth Vietnam could hardly be said to have been at peace from the moment that Gracey's forces first challenged Vietminh authority in Saigon in September 1945. Nor was it to know peace for another thirty years.

CHAPTER TWO

Colonial reconquest or Cold War conflict? The French war, 1946–54

In 1946, Ho Chi Minh predicted that a war between the Vietminh and the French would be a war between 'the tiger and the elephant'.

> If the tiger ever stands still the elephant will crush him with his mighty tusks. But the tiger does not stand still. He lurks in the jungle by day and emerges by night. He will leap upon the back of the elephant, tearing huge chunks from his hide, and then he will leap back into the dark jungle. And slowly the elephant will bleed to death.
>
> (Lacouture 1968, 138)

Over the next eight years, the accuracy of Ho's prediction would become apparent not only in the strategy employed by the Vietminh but, eventually, in the outcome of the war itself.

The opening phase of the conflict saw the French concentrate on consolidating their position in Cochinchina, something they accomplished by late 1947. In the north, the Vietminh, after a period of resistance in 1946–7, had withdrawn from all major urban centres to regroup in 'safe areas' in the mountains and countryside. From the outset, the Vietminh's strategy borrowed much from Mao Zedong and the Chinese communists who, in their contemporaneous conflict with the Guomindang, were waging a 'People's War'. According to Mao, the key to successful social revolution in countries like China (and, by inference, social *and* national revolution in colonial areas like Vietnam) lay in mobilizing the peasant masses. Peasant 'power' in support of revolutionary objectives would, Mao believed, create an irresistible force for change. So, too, did the Vietminh's communist leaders who, at the end of December 1946, formally adopted Mao's three-stage revolutionary methodology. The first stage was the creation of a liberated base area, something the Vietminh already possessed in embryonic form in the Viet Bac. The second involved a move to protracted guerrilla warfare. Although at the start of the war, Vietminh military forces totalled around 50,000, they were poorly armed and could not hope to take on and succeed against the well-equipped French forces in conventional set-piece engagements. The only alternative was to adopt a lower-level 'hit-and-run' approach (Ho's aggressive moving tiger philosophy) and to slowly but surely wear down the enemy. During this phase of the struggle, however, the emphasis would be as much political as military, with the rural masses and the smaller urban population targeted for recruitment purposes and primed for revolutionary action. The final stage would involve a move from guerrilla to conventional warfare and a general offensive throughout the country to seize power in the name of the people. If political preparations developed as planned, the people themselves would play a central role, participating in a widespread uprising to augment the final military push for victory. But in the specific context of Vietnam, there was an alternative road to victory, one that bypassed Mao's third stage, namely the prospect of a drawn-out guerrilla campaign leading to war-weariness in France and, ultimately, to a negotiated withdrawal on terms favourable to the Vietminh.

The French, for their part, initially assumed that their well-resourced army would easily crush the Vietminh. But in late 1947, the Vietminh began to wage guerrilla war in earnest. As they did, the French came to realize that superior firepower was of little use against an enemy who could not be brought to battle, and with this realization came an erosion of optimism about a swift victory. In the Viet Bac, the Vietminh were largely inaccessible, whilst in the countryside and the urban centres their military and political cadres were indistinguishable from the non-combatant population. Often the first the French knew of the Vietminh's presence was when the bullets began flying as the 'tiger' army attacked, drew blood, then melted away again. French prospects in the war were not helped by the refusal of successive governments in Paris to commit sufficient manpower, even when it became clear that the Vietminh were more resilient and better organized than anticipated. By the end of the 1940s, whilst the French were strong enough to defend the cities and towns, they lacked the means to mount sustained offensive operations aimed at destroying the Vietminh's rural primacy, still less to undertake an effective pacification programme. It has been estimated that by 1949 Vietminh military strength stood at around 250,000 men, giving it numerical parity with the French Expeditionary Force. But from the French standpoint, parity was not good enough. Conventional military wisdom suggested that the only way to defeat a guerrilla army was to overwhelm it with numbers. A ratio of 10:1 was considered the minimum requirement, but it was one that the French never got close to at any stage of the war. The demands of national defence, occupation duties in Germany and wider French Union security contributed to the impoverishment of the Expeditionary Force, but a reluctance to invest fully in a native Vietnamese army lest it metamorphose into a 'Frankenstein's monster' also played its part.

During 1948, the French attempted to ease their military difficulties by launching a political offensive against the Vietminh. Policy-makers in Paris were aware that the Vietminh's constituency included a great many non-communist nationalists who, faced with a choice between support for the French and a continuation of colonial rule, or support for the Vietminh and independence albeit under increasingly obvious communist direction, opted for the latter. If, however, Ho Chi Minh's hold over Vietnamese nationalism could be broken, the Vietminh's political *and* military potency might be broken as well. With this end in view, the French set about creating a Vietnamese 'government' to occupy the middle ground between colonialism and communism, one they hoped would encourage significant defections from the Vietminh. The former emperor of Annam, Bao Dai, was chosen to head the initiative, and on 8 March 1949 he and French President Vincent Auriol concluded the Elysée agreement. Under its terms, Vietnam was granted its independence as an Associated State within the French Union (Laos and Cambodia were later accorded the same status). The French also agreed to a unified Vietnam, ending Cochinchina's separation from Tonkin and Annam, the whole to fall under Bao Dai's jurisdiction.

Appearances were deceptive, however. In practice, the so-called Bao Dai 'solution' proved to be no solution at all, merely a case of the French tinkering with the detail rather than the substance of their rule. Under the new arrangement, France retained control of Vietnam's economy and its foreign and defence policy, forbade its secession from the French Union, and pointedly refused to provide a timetable by which this qualified independence would be perfected. In consequence,

21

the initiative was denounced as a colonial confidence trick by India and other independent Asian opinion, by the Communist bloc, and by dispassionate observers in the West. Nor did it lead to substantial defections from the Vietminh to the Bao Dai regime, whose popular base was confined to the affluent Saigon bourgeoisie and obvious anti-communist groupings, notably the country's two million Catholics. Even if non-communist adherents from the urban educated and professional class had changed sides in large numbers, Vietminh strength, rooted as it was in the countryside, would have remained strong. A peasant did not have to understand communist ideology to align himself with the Vietminh, only to know that Ho Chi Minh stood for easily comprehended patriotic goals, land reform and social justice. Thus, of the two Vietnams and the two native governments in existence from 1949, it was Ho's Democratic Republic, not Bao Dai's Associated State, that wielded the greater claim to represent the aspirations of the Vietnamese people as a whole.

Yet, for all its shortcomings, the Bao Dai experiment was still to have a profound impact on Vietnam and its future in that it enabled the United States to give open support to the French war effort. Hitherto, the Truman administration had kept its distance, put off by the strong colonial overtones of the struggle, but in May 1950 it inaugurated a military assistance programme which, by 1954, would be underwriting nearly 80 per cent of the total cost of the war. This massive commitment – totalling $2.6 billion in the 1950–4 period – was undertaken in the knowledge that Vietnamese independence under Bao Dai was a sham. What, then, caused the United States to abandon its anti-colonial stance? The answer, most historians now agree, is to be found in the evolving character of American national security policy in the early years of the Cold War.

The Soviet Union's occupation of Eastern Europe in 1945 destroyed the wartime Grand Alliance and gave rise to fears in Washington that Moscow planned to expand its power and influence throughout the rest of the continent, perhaps even into the Middle East and Asia. In formulating a response to this danger, the Truman administration appeared to face a stark choice: it could either go to war to free Eastern Europe and stem Soviet expansionism, or it could do nothing. Neither option had much to recommend it. The compromise strategy that emerged in 1946–7 was Containment, an acceptance of the Soviet sphere of influence as it stood, coupled with a determination to prevent any further communist gains at the expense of the 'free' world. Until the start of 1950, US Containment policy largely conformed to the precepts of its originator, George F. Kennan, one of the leading Soviet specialists in the Foreign Service. Taking the view that American military and economic resources were necessarily finite, Kennan drew a number of linked conclusions: 1) US objectives should always be related to the means to achieve them; 2) because means were limited, it followed that America could not contain communism everywhere but had instead to distinguish between vital areas to be defended at all costs and lesser ones that could be surrendered if necessary; 3) in this connection, there were only five truly vital parts of the world – the United States, the Soviet Union, Britain, Western Germany/Western Europe, and Japan – and that the principal aim of Containment should be to ensure that the four that were in 'friendly' hands stayed that way. Kennan also maintained that the Soviet Union would seek to extend its power not by direct military means but by political, diplomatic and economic methods, and by taking advantage of opportunities offered by Western weakness or division.

The Truman administration's initial allegiance to Kennanite Containment helps explain its refusal to become drawn into the French war in Vietnam: Western Europe, a vital interest, made the greatest claims on American attention and resources before 1949, whilst Vietnam was a side-show in Kennanite terms. There was, in addition, a strong conviction in US policy-making circles that the French, in concert with the British in Malaya and Singapore, should be capable on their own of dealing with peasant-based communism in Southeast Asia. Above all, Americans were loath to identify themselves too closely with European colonialism. Officially, therefore, the United States was neutral during the early years of the Franco–Vietminh war. But, unofficially, the last thing Washington wanted was the replacement of a colonial regime by a communist one. The Truman administration consequently turned a blind eye as significant amounts of financial and military aid, ostensibly supplied for use in Europe, were redirected by the French to Indochina. However, what the French really needed was open and major rather than covert and limited US support.

Paris pursued this objective in two ways. First, the Bao Dai 'solution', by diluting the colonial character of the war, was intended to make it easier for Washington to provide the necessary aid. Second, following the enunciation of the Truman Doctrine in March 1947, the

French went out of their way to stress the Vietminh's communist complexion so as to elicit sympathy from the growing anti-communist consensus in America. Initially, however, the Bao Dai gambit misfired, with the Truman administration deeply suspicious of French motives and sincerity. Yet, on 7 February 1950, and without the French adding to Bao Dai's authority, the United States extended formal diplomatic recognition to Vietnam as an independent state within the French Union. This was quickly followed in May by the commencement of public and direct military assistance, with a start-up appropriation of $10 million. To many historians, these decisions mark the first fateful step on the road to full US military involvement in Vietnam in the 1960s – the road, that was, to America's longest war and to America's most humiliating defeat. For, crucially, from May 1950 onwards, Vietnam's non-communist future was no longer a matter of purely French prestige and credibility, it had become a vital American concern, too.

This deeply portentous change in US policy owed much to the interaction of major international developments with American domestic politics. In September 1949, the Soviet Union successfully tested an atomic bomb and, in the process, destroyed the American atomic monopoly. Then, the following month, came the final triumph of Mao Zedong's communists in the Chinese civil war and the birth of the People's Republic of China (**PRC**). Within the Truman administration, fears mounted that international communism was on the verge of a new aggressive and expansionist phase. The reaction of American public opinion to these disturbing developments added to the administration's problems. A domestic political firestorm engulfed the government, which was variously accused of passing atomic secrets to the Soviets, of abandoning or betraying the nationalist Chinese leader Chiang Kai-shek, and of being soft on communism in general and on Asian communism in particular. The flames were fanned by the Republicans, out of office since 1933 and keen to discredit the Democrats in any way possible, with the most extreme attacks coming from Senator Joseph R. McCarthy and his followers on the far right of the party.

Prompted by the worrying situation abroad and by the need to disarm critics at home, Truman ordered a major review of his administration's entire national security policy. The result was presented to him in April 1950 as National Security Council paper #68 (**NSC-68**). In approving both its analysis and recommendations, Truman was to break decisively with Kennanite Containment and move, equally decisively, towards closer involvement in Vietnam. NSC-68 argued that Soviet expansionism was ideologically driven, that Moscow was working to a blueprint for world domination, and that it was now possessed of the power to further its ambition by force. To combat this heightened danger, the document's authors insisted that the United States had to dramatically increase defence spending to enhance its nuclear arsenal, forge ahead with development of a hydrogen bomb, and build up its previously run-down conventional armed forces. Above all, Containment had to be universalized, with no differentiation between vital and non-vital interests. Kennan's key power centres, the study maintained, could not be defended without defending the areas surrounding them, a conclusion that had obvious implications for US policy towards Vietnam. By institutionalizing what would later be called the domino theory, NSC-68 accorded the French colony a strategic importance it had previously lacked and led, in May 1950, to the start of open US military assistance to France. Anti-communism had triumphed over anti-colonialism in American foreign policy formulation. Henceforth, US policy-makers would view Vietnam as a Cold War problem, pure and simple.

The North Korean attack on South Korea in June 1950 appeared to confirm the validity of NSC-68's assumptions and led Washington to view the conflict in Vietnam as one wing of a general Asian front against co-ordinated Soviet–Chinese aggression, with Formosa the other wing and Korea located in the centre. It also led to a substantial increase in US military aid to France in Vietnam. By the end of 1950, the initial appropriation of $10 million had grown to $100 million, and an American Military Assistance Advisory Group (**MAAG**) had been established in Saigon to oversee the programme. Even so, US war material was slow in reaching its destination and, by late 1950, it was another external power, China, that was making the greater impact in Vietnam. With the creation of the People's Republic of China in 1949, the Vietminh was provided with a powerful and geographically-proximate fraternal ally, and though Communist China and the Soviet Union both extended full diplomatic recognition to the Democratic Republic of Vietnam in January 1950, Moscow was evidently happy to let the Chinese take the lead in supporting the Vietnamese revolution (Qiang Zhai 1993a, 693). Ho Chi Minh embarked on a series of meetings with PRC leaders, eventually securing Chinese agreement to furnish arms and military advisers to the Vietminh army. General

Giap's forces now totalled 200,000 regulars, with over a million local and regional guerrillas in support roles, but were poorly equipped and still novices in the art of 'People's War'. By the autumn of 1950, the value of Beijing's assistance was made clear when, in a major offensive conceived and directed by Chinese General Chen Geng, the French were defeated at Dongkhe, Caobang and Langson and so lost control of the vital border area between northern Tonkin and China. As a result, the Vietminh obtained unimpeded access to their new bene-factor, a mountain of abandoned military supplies and, for the first time in the war, the military initiative.[1]

In December 1950, in the wake of the French disaster in Tonkin, Paris appointed General Jean de Lattre de Tassigny as commander in Indochina. A hero of the Second World War, de Lattre's inspiring leadership helped restore both the morale of the French Expeditionary Force and the military balance. Early in 1951, the Vietminh, buoyed up by the success of their autumn border campaign, launched a large-scale regular-unit assault on the French position around Hanoi and the Red River delta only to be badly mauled, losing around 6,000 men. If, as is sometimes suggested, this operation was seen by the Vietminh's communist leadership as the beginning of the general offensive stage of their revolution, it was clearly premature and they were forced to revert to attritional guerrilla tactics. In the international arena, de Lattre worked tirelessly to present the conflict as a wholly Cold War problem, but with his death from cancer in January 1952 French mili-tary fortunes went into decline once more. The Vietminh expanded and consolidated their hold on rural Tonkin, forcing the French to retire behind a defence perimeter in the lower Red River delta encom-passing Hanoi and Haiphong, but it proved a hopelessly porous barrier to enemy infiltration.

These Vietminh advances occurred in spite of the decision by Ho Chi Minh and his advisers to re-establish an overtly communist orga-nization in Vietnam. The Indochinese Communist Party had been disbanded in November 1945 as a concession to the anti-communist sensibilities of the Guomindang, then in occupation of northern Vietnam. In February 1951, however, the communists moved into the open once more with the formation of the Vietnamese Workers' Party

---

[1]Over the next four years, the Vietminh was to receive about 80,000 tons of military supplies from China (including 116,000 guns and 4,630 cannons), roughly the equivalent of $700 million-worth of aid (Qiang Zhai 1993a, *passim*).

(**VWP**) and its subsequent domination of both the Vietminh and DRV government posts.[2] It may have been Soviet and Chinese diplomatic recognition of the Democratic Republic that brought about this open declaration of ideological allegiance, but regardless of the motivation, the emergence of the VWP signalled that the Vietnamese national revolution would, for the first time since the creation of the Vietminh ten years earlier, move forward within an avowedly Marxist-Leninist framework (Duiker 1996, 149). Some non-communist defections followed, but the lack of legitimacy of the Bao Dai alternative, together with the indisputable patriotism of the Vietminh (even if communist-led), ensured continuing and widespread support. In the countryside, meanwhile, land redistribution and rent reductions in Vietminh 'liberated' areas clearly played a big part in retaining peasant loyalty.

The main constraint on French military effectiveness in 1952–3 continued to be lack of manpower which, in turn, produced a defensive strategy. A native Vietnamese army had at last come into being, totalling approximately 100,000 by 1953, but it was under-employed by a French High Command contemptuous of its ability. Troops from other parts of the French Union, particularly North Africa, were recruited to the Expeditionary Force in increasing numbers, but their martial ardour was likewise questioned by their commanders. French conscripts were prevented by law from participating in theatres of active operations in times of 'general peace', thus denying the French in Vietnam a source of manpower which the British were putting to good use in dealing with a communist insurgency in Malaya. This left the regular French army in Europe as the only quality source of reinforcement, but as of late 1952 this consisted of just five full-strength divisions, five in formation and two still to be created. So the French battled on, with scant prospect of extra troops from Europe and little certainty even that losses would be made good. By mid-1953, the French Expeditionary Force totalled 500,000, of which a staggering seventy per cent were tied down in static defence, whilst Vietminh force levels exceeded 300,000 and had far fewer restrictions on their mobility (Hess 1990, 41; Duiker 1996, 163). In France itself, political and popular opinion grew increasingly disenchanted with the war. American aid notwithstanding, the war had cost more than twice the

---

[2]Separate but related offshoots were established in Laos and Cambodia, thus the Vietnam Worker's Party was not a straight reincarnation of the defunct Indochinese Communist Party.

amount France had received for its economic revival under the Marshall Plan. The human cost, however, was greater in all senses: in 1952, the French lost more young officers in Indochina than the total number of graduates produced by the St Cyr military academy over the previous four years, and by mid-1953 combined French and French Union casualties were reported to be close to 150,000. The negative tactics forced on the Expeditionary Force by limited manpower only added to disillusionment in France: static defence provided the Vietminh with easy targets, and every time an attack succeeded and lives were lost, public and parliamentary gloom increased. By 1953, therefore, the French position was threatened not only by Vietminh military success, but by growing enthusiasm in metropolitan France for a negotiated solution. Moreover, in their steadfast refusal to publish a timetable by which Vietnam would become fully independent, the French ensured that Ho Chi Minh rather than Bao Dai continued to be seen by the majority of the politically-conscious native population as the only genuine nationalist alternative, a political omission that compounded the military problem.

This was the reality of the situation. But the French governments of the period refused to accept it as such and remained stubbornly committed to victory, at least when discussing increased assistance with the Americans who, not surprisingly, sought some assurance that their investment would achieve results. In particular, Washington pressed for an enlightened political policy and a more forward military strategy, but the French, whilst happy to take American aid, allowed no interference in their conduct of the war. The French knew that they were fighting as much for American Cold War objectives as they were for their own national and colonial interests. And the Americans knew it too, hence their inability – and unwillingness – to attach firm conditions to the continuation of their military aid programme.

This said, for a time in the summer of 1953 the new Republican administration of Dwight D. Eisenhower appeared to have achieved a breakthrough. With Congressional discontent mounting, the French were told that further American aid would depend on them producing a strategic and political plan for winning the war. On 3 July, French Premier Joseph Laniel responded by publicly declaring his government's readiness to open negotiations with representatives of all three Associated States with the aim of completing their independence. Two weeks later, the French commander in Vietnam, General Henri Navarre, announced his determination to take the war to the enemy and, to this end, to greatly expand the Vietnamese army which would, in due course, become the principal vehicle for offensive operations. In September, satisfied that Paris had done what had been asked of it, President Eisenhower approved a further $385 million of military aid above and beyond the $400 million already committed for 1953–4. But all was not as it seemed. The Franco–Associated States talks collapsed almost as soon as they started, the French continuing to deny the right of secession from the French Union, the minimum demand of even moderate nationalists. Nor, on closer inspection, did the Navarre Plan measure up to expectations. Aside from his commitment to developing the Vietnamese army, Navarre had asked Paris for reinforcements from the metropolitan French army to the tune of twelve battalions. He was eventually promised nine, but received only seven, almost all of North African derivation. Approaching the new campaigning season, therefore, the forces at Navarre's disposal were barely adequate to hold the existing position, never mind mount major offensive operations. What Washington had thought of as a strategy for victory turned out to be a strategy for negotiation, as the French political establishment, with a few obstinate exceptions, came to conclude that a compromise settlement offered the best way out of the war. However, to ensure a strong bargaining position when the time came, France had to fight on to a position of military strength. To retain the good offices of the United States, this limited objective was packaged as an all-out effort.

The potential for a peaceful solution increased in November 1953 when Ho Chi Minh declared himself ready to negotiate a settlement, a move that excited French opinion and placed the government in Paris under pressure to explore the sincerity of his offer. The reverberations from Ho's statement were felt in Berlin in February 1954, at a four-power (America, Britain, France and the Soviet Union) Foreign Minister's conference. When, predictably, the four delegations failed to resolve their differences over the main agenda item, Germany, they agreed to convene a further conference in Geneva in April on the post-armistice future of Korea. However, Georges Bidault, the French Foreign Minister, responding to domestic pressures, lobbied hard and ultimately successfully for the inclusion of Vietnam as a discussion item on the Geneva agenda. The cost, though, was a rift with the Americans, who were deeply sceptical about the prospects of fruitful discussions on Vietnam given the weakness of the French military position there.

The two months leading up to the Geneva conference saw both the French and the Vietminh attempt to improve their respective negotiating prospects through success on the battlefield, in particular at the looming battle for Dienbienphu, a valley in north-west Tonkin occupied by the French in November 1953. In building a fortress at Dienbienphu, the French military hoped to entice the Vietminh into a set-piece battle on terms and terrain that were, for once, of their own choosing. At first, the Vietminh declined to be drawn into the trap, some 35,000 troops simply digging-in on the hills surrounding the valley. But following the decision to hold the Geneva conference, General Giap, working closely with Chinese advisers, ordered offensive preparations to begin. American military experts who visited the redoubt on the eve of the battle believed it could be held against all-comers, but they, and the French, had seriously underestimated the ingenuity of the Vietminh.

This was instantly apparent when the battle opened on 13 March 1954 with a heavy artillery bombardment, for the French had assumed that the Vietminh would be unable to get their heavy long-range guns into a position from which to target the garrison. But the Vietminh, using tens of thousands of peasant volunteers, had dismantled their weaponry and transported it up into the hills piece-by-piece where it was reassembled and then camouflaged to avoid detection. Among the earliest targets of the gunners was the airstrip, the garrison's lifeline, which was quickly put out of action. Thereafter supplies had to be parachuted in, a high-risk undertaking in the face of anti-aircraft fire and often poor visibility, and a significant percentage fell – literally – into Vietminh hands. The initial bombardment had been followed by human-wave frontal assaults, costly to the French but far costlier to the Vietminh, and Giap soon abandoned the tactic in defiance of his Chinese advisers who had suggested it in the first place. At the end of March, the Vietminh opted to lay siege to the fortress whilst gradually whittling away at its defensive perimeter, eventually pitting 49,500 combatants and 55,000 support troops against the 16,000-man garrison.

In Washington, the Eisenhower administration contemplated how best to react to the fast-deteriorating situation. The main American concern was that the fall of Dienbienphu would so energize the Vietminh and so demoralize the French as to threaten the collapse of the entire non-communist position throughout Vietnam and possibly even Southeast Asia, a worry given public expression by Eisenhower when he coined the term 'domino theory' to describe the likely consequences of a French defeat. Almost as disturbing from the American viewpoint was the possibility of a French capitulation at the forthcoming Geneva conference. What could the United States do to prevent a breach in the Containment barrier in Southeast Asia and a breach in Western unity at Geneva? When it came to considering a possible military solution, the key decision-makers were mostly split into interventionists and non-interventionists. Occupying the middle ground was President Eisenhower, the decisive figure in the equation. Whilst not opposed to military action *per se*, Eisenhower did want to ensure that objectives were clear and attainable and that the American commitment in Vietnam was limited to air and sea. He also insisted on exhaustive political preparation, in particular Congressional backing, though he understood that this would depend on the administration securing the widest possible allied support for intervention and, from the French, an unequivocal promise of independence for Vietnam once the war was over. At the end of March, therefore, the US government rejected any thought of unilateral airstrikes against the Vietminh at Dienbienphu, as well as the tentatively explored possibility of employing tactical nuclear weapons, and decided instead to issue a public appeal to its allies for 'united action' to prevent the 'imposition on Southeast Asia of the political system of Communist Russia and its Chinese Communist ally' (Folliot 1957, 144–5).

In retrospect, the US government had erected near-insurmountable barriers to military action. On 3 April, Congressional leaders reacted much as the President had predicted in expressing their disapproval of measures that buttressed European colonialism or led the United States to assume the main burden in a supposedly 'free world' enterprise. The first problem was that the French remained adamantly opposed to unfettered independence for Vietnam, and seemed to hope that Cold War considerations would bring about unconditional American intervention. This hope might have been realized but for the second problem: nothing came of 'united action'. Strategists in Washington had envisioned a coalition comprising the United States, Britain, France, Australia and New Zealand, together with the prowestern Asian governments of Thailand, the Philippines and the three Associated States, that would intervene to shore up the French position beyond Dienbienphu (by early April American observers, unlike the French, had concluded that the garrison was beyond saving). From the start, it was evident that the support of America's closest ally, Britain, was critical to the success of 'united action'. Britain, after all, maintained a significant military presence in Southeast Asia, particularly in Malaya and Singapore, and had been singled out by Congressional leaders as a key factor in deciding their final attitude to the administration's plans. But Churchill's Conservative government, after much consideration, decided to set itself against a military solution to the problem. The risks inherent in 'united action' were, in Foreign Secretary Anthony Eden's judgement, too great: American or American-led intervention might provoke Chinese *counter*-intervention on the Korean model, trigger a general conflagration across Asia, activate the Sino–Soviet mutual security pact of 1950, invite Soviet atomic strikes against US bases in East Anglia, and lead ultimately to a 'third world war'. With the Geneva conference about to explore the potential for peace in Vietnam, the British would not endorse what Churchill called 'a policy which might lead by slow stages to a catastrophe' (Ruane 1996, 141–2).

In the light of the negative reaction of London and Paris, some historians have argued that Eisenhower established the pre-conditions for 'united action' in the certain knowledge that they would not be met. In other words, the US government privately accepted that intervention could not save the French, but to avoid domestic accusations of communist appeasement it engineered a situation whereby the blame for inaction would fall on the British and the French. The Americans certainly *talked* of intervention throughout the crisis but, the argument goes, this was a calculated effort to create uncertainty in Beijing and Moscow about ultimate US intentions and so help secure a reasonable political settlement at Geneva. However, while falling short of providing a conclusive rebuttal to this theory, research in recent years does suggest a seriousness of intent in Washington in 1954, and that military action was likely if the conditions warranted it and the proper arrangements could be made (Ruane 1996, 168). It is clear, moreover, that the Americans felt badly let down by the British, and relations between the two countries deteriorated rapidly, reaching their nadir when the Geneva conference finally opened on 26 April 1954. The British delegation, taking US threats of military action at face value, sought to eliminate the danger of a new, wider and potentially nuclear war by finding a negotiated solution to the present and still limited one. In contrast, the American team displayed scant enthusiasm for the conference, snubbed the Chinese, insisted on observer rather than formal participant status, and continued to make menacing 'noises off' about military action.

From 26 April to 8 May, Korea was the formal focus of attention at Geneva. The fall of Dienbienphu on 7 May overshadowed the first session on Vietnam: during the fifty-five day battle, the French lost 1,500 men killed, 4,000 wounded and 10,000 taken prisoner, while Vietminh casualties amounted to some 8,000 dead and 15,000 wounded (Clayton 1994, 71*ff*; Duiker 1996, 170). In the ensuing negotiations, Eden and Soviet Foreign Minister Vyachaslav Molotov, co-chairmen of the conference, were confronted with an understandably ebullient Vietminh; a forlorn but stubborn French delegation that hoped to avoid the ignominy of a diplomatic defeat in the wake of their military humiliation; representatives of the three Associated States of Indochina, less than happy about the French negotiating on their behalf; a still embittered American team that teased the French about military intervention and generally contributed little of value to the proceedings; and the Chinese communists, enjoying their first international conference but keeping their intentions to themselves. For a month, Eden and Molotov, united in their desire to defuse a potential catalyst for general war, sought to create the basis for a peaceful settlement only to find the task beyond them. By early June, the conference faced collapse, while continued Vietminh advances in Tonkin threatened the French position in Hanoi and, inevitably, kept alive the question of American military action.

The peace process was saved, however, when Pierre Mendès-France formed a government in France that was, for the first time, unequivocally committed to a political solution. A long-time critic of the war, Mendès-France determined to obtain a cease-fire within a month or resign, a deadline that translated as 20 July 1954. The Chinese, possibly fearing the military consequences in Vietnam of a diplomatic failure in Switzerland, and seeing in the new French administration the potential for a satisfactory compromise, suddenly adopted a more conciliatory tone in the negotiations. Together, these developments made some kind of agreement possible and, since the United States could hardly intervene without the permission of the French, removed any lingering danger of a wider war. What was not removed, however, was the potential for American spoiling tactics. As the conference inched towards agreement on the basis of the partition of Vietnam, the US delegation made clear that it would not sign any treaty that surrendered territory to communism. Since the key to success at Geneva was compromise, and compromise meant some concessions to the strength of the Vietminh's position, this amounted to a refusal to sign anything. The representatives of the Associated State of Vietnam followed the American lead. So, too, did the Soviets and the Chinese, neither of whom wished to be committed to an arrangement that did not bind the United States. With the Mendès-France deadline fast approaching, Eden, personally dedicated to the nascent settlement, was again confronted with the collapse of the conference. Working on the premise that a flawed solution was better than no solution, Eden arranged for a 'declaration' to be issued instead of a conventional treaty, prefaced by a heading in which all participating parties would be listed and outlining the arrangements arrived at by the conference. Nothing would be signed other than cease-fire articles on the spot in Indochina.

On 21 July 1954, a few hours after the expiry of the French deadline, the conference ended in a measure of harmony. Under the Geneva accords, cease-fires were arranged for Vietnam, as well as Laos and Cambodia, their provisions to be monitored by an International Supervisory Commission comprising India, Poland and Canada. The introduction of foreign troops into all three Indochinese states was prohibited, thus neutralizing the whole area. In Laos, the Royal government was obliged to come to terms with the communist Pathet Lao (then in possession of around 50 per cent of Laotian territory) and to create an integrated administration, though no such demand was made of the Cambodian government in respect of the smaller communist Khmer Issarak. Vietnam was to be divided at the 17th parallel into two zones, with the Vietminh regrouping in the north and the French and Bao Dai forces in the south. The civilian population was to be free to settle either side of the partition line. Neither zone was permitted to join a military alliance or allow foreign military bases on its soil. This division of Vietnam was, however, provisional. As the final declaration made unmistakably clear, the demarcation line 'should not in any way be interpreted as constituting a political or territorial boundary'. Internationally-supervised nation-wide elections were to be held in July 1956, after which Vietnam's unity would be restored and its independence completed. The French agreed to retain military forces in the southern zone until the 1956 poll, unless asked to withdraw earlier by the Bao Dai regime (McMahon 1995, 124–5).

These are the bare bones of the settlement. But who gained and who lost? The French were rid of a damaging eight-year war with a measure of honour intact; partition at the 17th parallel was generous considering the post-Dienbienphu military strength of the Vietminh who, in agreeing to that line, retroceded twenty per cent of territory and 1.5 million people under their jurisdiction (Lacouture 1968, 154). As for the Vietminh, it now appears that they might have held out for more advantageous terms, but the Chinese and Soviets, both of whom were nervous about the American reaction if the war dragged on, pressurized them into accepting the ones on offer. For China, the final settlement had particular attractions: it enhanced the security of its southern border, and offered the prospect of an extended buffer zone through a Vietminh victory in the 1956 election; it avoided a wider conflict and so allowed the PRC to concentrate on much-needed internal reconstruction; and there was, in addition, a potential diplomatic pay-off for its moderation at Geneva in the shape of international support for its admission to the United Nations. The Vietminh, though less than happy with the agreement, acquiesced in the interests of international communist solidarity. When, however, Vietnam and the PRC went to war in 1979, Hanoi published the so-called 'White Book' which, if it is to be trusted, confirmed both China's 'betrayal' at Geneva and the dismay of many in the Vietminh at having to settle for compromise when total victory appeared within their grasp (Smith 1983, I, 24, 59–60). Ho Chi Minh's motives in supporting the settlement remain unclear. As a realist, he may have concluded that a staggered victory was preferable to the prolongation of a war that had already cost the Vietnamese up to 500,000 lives, its possible expansion through American intervention, increased Vietminh reliance on Beijing at the expense of its cherished autonomy, and maybe even defeat. But the Chinese may also have insisted on his acquiescence as a *quid pro quo* for the weaponry that brought success at Dienbienphu. Either way, Ho's approval contributed to – albeit reluctant – Vietminh acceptance.

The British could be well-satisfied with their contribution to the outcome at Geneva: Eden's patient determination helped keep the conference alive so that when the central players were finally ready to negotiate seriously, they had a ready-made forum within which to reach agreement. In general, Geneva was a victory for Britain's flexible and pragmatic approach to Communist China over the American predilection for provocation and diplomatic ostracism. The least happy participants in the drama were the Associated States of Vietnam and, in public at any rate, the United States. The furthest the

Eisenhower administration would go in endorsing the accords was to agree to refrain from the threat or use of force to disturb them. Privately, however, the Americans viewed the Geneva *dénouement* as rather better than they had once feared. After all, only the northern half of the Vietnamese 'domino' had been lost when, at one time, it looked as though the whole country would have to be surrendered. Moreover, there was still the prospect of preserving southern Vietnam, and in the unsigned final declaration of the Geneva conference there was the opportunity to do so without violating a binding international treaty. As Eden conceded in winding-up the conference, everything now depended on the 'spirit' in which Geneva's provisions were followed through, an appeal which, in the light of subsequent events, perhaps ought to have been addressed specifically to Washington and Saigon.

CHAPTER THREE

Nation building: North and South Vietnam, 1954–61

In the aftermath of the Geneva conference, the United States government determined to create a stable anti-communist state in southern Vietnam. Quite how 'nation building', as this approach would become known, could proceed without violating the spirit of Geneva was unclear, but this mattered less to Washington than the containment of further communist expansion in Southeast Asia. Besides, as the Eisenhower administration was wont to point out, it had signed nothing at Geneva that obligated it to uphold the settlement. The government of the southern-based State of Vietnam adopted a similar attitude and, in the person of its Prime Minister, Ngo Dinh Diem, the United States found a more than willing accomplice in its efforts to circumvent the accords. Diem – an ardent Catholic, a fervent nationalist and a staunch anti-communist – had spent the last years of the Franco–Vietminh war in the United States cultivating political support for himself and a version of Vietnamese nationalism that denied the legitimacy of both the Vietminh and Bao Dai varieties. Early in 1954, he came to the attention of US policy-makers who, it has been suggested, were so impressed by his militant anti-communism that they worked to ensure his elevation to the Premiership in Saigon. If true, rewards were soon forthcoming as Diem's refusal to endorse the Geneva settlement made the American abstention all the easier to justify. In spite of the doubts of some senior figures in the Eisenhower administration concerning his illiberal and autocratic tendencies, Diem went on to become the standard-bearer for 'nation building'. Diem might not have been the perfect democrat in 1954, but given time and the right advice, US policy-makers believed that this failing could be rectified.

First, however, the foundations of 'nation building' had to be laid. An early priority was to remove the French who were keen to retain political and economic influence in southern Vietnam. To the Americans, even vestigial colonialism threatened the success of 'nation building', and the French soon found themselves under pressure to relinquish their remaining foothold. In October 1954, President Eisenhower approved the extension of US military and economic assistance directly to Diem's government, bypassing the French through whom it had previously been channelled. In January 1955, Diem assumed complete political authority from the residual colonial administration and declared that his country's independence was now a reality. The following month, Washington undertook full responsibility for the financing and training of the South Vietnamese armed forces. Finally, in April 1956, the last French troops left Vietnam. 'We have a clean base there now, without the taint of colonialism', declared John Foster Dulles, the US Secretary of State. Dienbienphu had been 'a blessing in disguise' (Young 1991, 46).

Alongside its anti-French manoeuvrings, the Eisenhower administration sought to create political stability below the 17th parallel by manufacturing political instability above it. Orchestrating operations was Colonel Edward Lansdale, Head of the US Military Mission in Saigon. Under Lansdale's direction, teams of trained anti-communist Vietnamese were sent north to engage in acts of sabotage. Their greatest success, however, was in igniting rumours of imminent communist retribution against anyone who had opposed the Vietminh during the war with France. As a result, an estimated 900,000 people fled south in the first months after partition, the majority of them Catholics fearful of persecution, and Washington and Saigon made considerable propaganda capital out what was portrayed as an exodus from tyranny. At the same time, around 130,000 northern-based French forces regrouped in the south, with about the same number of Vietminh troops and supporters moving in the opposite direction. For Diem, the influx of half a million Catholics – swelling the Catholic community in southern Vietnam to about 1 million, or just under 10 per cent of the total population – was important in helping to broaden a political power-base hitherto confined to Vietnamese who had served in the army or colonial bureaucracy during French rule, the affluent urban bourgeoisie, large rural landowners and the southern-born Catholic population.

On the international scene, the Eisenhower administration took steps to ensure that southern Vietnam, as well as Laos and Cambodia, came within the remit of the South East Asia Treaty Organization (**SEATO**), formed in September 1954. SEATO brought together the United States, Britain, Australia, New Zealand, Thailand, Pakistan and the Philippines in an alliance intended to deter or repel 'external' communist aggression in the Southeast Asian region. By a separate American-sponsored protocol, southern Vietnam, Laos and Cambodia were given SEATO protection without themselves formally acceding to the treaty, a piece of diplomatic alchemy that upheld the letter though not the spirit of the Geneva neutrality clauses. The Americans found it harder, however, to get their SEATO partners to agree to action in the event of 'internal' communist subversion. According to the Final Declaration of the Geneva conference, partition of Vietnam was a temporary division of a single country, thus if the north either attacked the south or promoted a southern-based communist insurgency, it could hardly be said to be external aggression. On the contrary, it would amount to a civil war, and America's SEATO allies expressed deep reservations about interference in internal Vietnamese affairs. The Eisenhower administration responded by claiming that two separate Vietnamese states had been created in July 1954, a fiction it adhered to throughout the rest of the decade. It was, moreover, on this basis – the defence of one country, South Vietnam, against the allegedly aggressive designs of another, North Vietnam – that the massive American military intervention of the 1960s would largely be justified.

At the start of 1955, with French influence waning and the SEATO protocol in place, the Eisenhower administration believed it had gone some way towards ensuring the immediate future of southern Vietnam. In contrast, Diem's prospects seemed less certain. In the autumn of 1954, in an attempt to consolidate his hold on power, Diem had set about neutralizing his non-communist opponents only to find them stronger and more numerous than anticipated. Gradually, however, he mastered the situation, and his triumph was sealed in October 1955 by an overwhelming (but almost certainly rigged) victory over Bao Dai in a referendum to choose a President to lead a new Republic of Vietnam (**RVN**) that claimed, like its Hanoi-based counterpart, the Democratic Republic of Vietnam, to encompass and so represent the whole of the country. A new constitution was promulgated and an RVN National Assembly elected in 1956, but Diem so manipulated the system that the reins of effective executive authority remained firmly in his hands. Ultimately, however, Diem's success owed a great deal to the Eisenhower administration. It was American money, for example, that helped buy the support of the Cao Dai and Hoa Hao, politico-religious sects with four million adherents between them, while it was Eisenhower's personal emissary, General J. Lawton Collins, who helped thwart the plans of anti-Diemist army officers by making clear that US aid, including money for the army payroll, was dependent upon Diem's continuance in office. These interventions ensured that Washington's 'man' eventually came through, but some US policy-makers feared that the power struggle had served to strengthen Diem's already marked preference for centralizing power in the hands of himself and a small circle of loyal advisers, an unfortunate development as far as the new Republic's democratic development was concerned.

The last remaining obstacle in the path of nation building was the all-Vietnam elections. Scheduled for July 1956, few knowledgeable observers doubted that they would be won by the Vietminh. There was some worry in Washington about a violent North Vietnamese reaction if the elections were aborted, but the risks attendant on abandonment were considered less than those that would be run if the poll went ahead. Thus there were few American complaints when Diem refused to take part in a north–south election co-ordinating conference in July 1955 and continued, over the next twelve months, to make abundantly clear his opposition to the elections themselves. Both Saigon and Washington justified their position by arguing, once again, that they had signed nothing at Geneva and could not be bound by its provisions, and by claiming that because the north was controlled by the communists it followed that the elections would only be truly 'free' in the south. Whilst some historians emphasize the technical legality of the American interpretation of Geneva, others are more critical, arguing that the United States conspired to deny the Vietnamese the opportunity to decide their own political future and, in so doing, betrayed one of the guiding principles of its foreign policy, namely the right of all peoples to national self-determination. Either way, the consequence was the same – twenty more years of war, not only for Vietnam but for America as well.

In North Vietnam, meanwhile, a different kind of 'nation building' was taking place. In October 1954, Ho Chi Minh and his comrades had re-entered Hanoi for the first time in nearly eight years. In the newly legitimized Democratic Republic of Vietnam, all political power resided in the Vietnamese Workers' Party (VWP). The principal decision-making body was the Politburo, whose dozen members also occupied the chief governmental positions. Ho, for example, was President of the DRV; Pham Van Dong – a founder member of the Indochinese Communist Party in 1930 – was, from 1955, the DRV's Prime Minister; and General Giap was both DRV Defence Minister and, after 1955, a Deputy Premier. All major decisions reached by the Politburo had to be approved by the Central Committee, a larger executive body elected by the VWP National Congress to effect policy on its behalf during the periods (normally five years) between Congresses. The Central Committee had expanded *pari passu* with the growth of the Party's membership until it became too cumbersome a vehicle for policy-making, hence the creation of the smaller Politburo. Once a decision was taken in the Politburo and endorsed in the Central Committee, the Leninist principle of 'democratic centralism' took over, with members at all lower levels of the Party apparatus expected to obey unswervingly the dictates of the leadership, translating them into action on a local, provincial and regional scale.

There was a remarkable continuity in the composition of the VWP hierarchy. In 1954, the Politburo comprised nearly all the men who, in 1945, had declared Vietnam independent and who would, from the mid-1960s, oversee the war with the United States. This is not to say that there were never differences between the leaders, indeed there is evidence to suggest that disagreements were sometimes profound. But respect for overall Party unity ensured ultimate allegiance to whatever compromise decision emerged. The debate over the merits of the Geneva settlement seems to have followed this pattern. A significant body of opinion considered the terms far less favourable than the Vietminh's political and military strength in 1954 deserved. Le Duan, a southerner and a rising star of the Party, was the chief Politburo critic of Geneva. He argued that instead of accepting a deficient peace agreement, the post-Dienbienphu military momentum should have been built upon to secure total victory, and he now favoured a strategy aimed at retrieving what had been lost. But what Le Duan ignored, and Ho Chi Minh emphasized, was that the alternative to acceptance of Geneva was to fight on, not just against France but probably the United States as well. And, if their attitude at Geneva was anything to go by, to fight on without any assurance of Soviet or Chinese backing. Conceding the force of this argument, Le Duan and the other militants fell in with the rest of the Party leadership in agreeing that the immediate priority was to consolidate the revolution in the north.

Because of the country's primitive economic–industrial base, however, the construction of a socialist state in North Vietnam proved in practice to be an evolutionary rather than a revolutionary process. As early as July 1954, a DRV government directive, in announcing plans to nationalize a number of large concerns previously run by the French but otherwise respect private wealth and property, signalled that economic development would occur initially within the framework of a mixed economy. In other words, the existing capitalist structure would be utilized to build the economic foundations upon which socialism would rest in the future. The directive was designed to reassure those non-communist northerners with capital, property or wealth-generating potential that they had nothing to fear under a communist regime, but it evidently failed for it was precisely these people who chose to migrate south in large numbers in the months after Geneva.

The most urgent post-partition problem confronting the DRV was a critical food shortage. Collectivization, the obvious ideological approach to the rural economy, was rejected by Hanoi in favour of a more pragmatic and immediately effective means of increasing the production of rice, the staple food crop. Beginning in early 1955, the Party's land reform programme sanctioned the confiscation of holdings belonging to the largest landlords and their redistribution amongst the landless and poorer peasants. Encouraged by the prospect of selling the surplus of their labours in the market place, it was intended that these newly landed peasants would contribute to heightened rice output. Meanwhile, the property of those categorized as 'middle' peasants (those possessing moderate-sized holdings) was exempted from the programme, a concession designed – like the efforts taken to appease the land hunger of the poorer peasants – to cement rural support for the revolution. Results, however, were decidedly mixed. On the positive side, more than 2 million acres were redistributed and rice production increased from 2.6 million tons in 1954 to 4.2 million tons in 1956, just about sufficient for the needs of the population (Hess 1990, 64). More negatively, the doctrinaire cadres who implemented policy in the field seem to have seen their task as the liquidation of all but the poorest peasants, and the process quickly gained a bloody momentum that the Party leadership was hard-pressed to check. Historians differ greatly over the number of people who lost their lives during the land reform period (ranging from a low of 3,000 to a high of more than 100,000), but there is little dispute that a great many innocent people were the victims of incorrect categorization. In August 1956, even Ho Chi Minh, in otherwise extolling the success of the initiative, conceded that 'errors' had been committed and announced that the more zealous cadres would be punished, the pace of reform slowed, and efforts made to reconstruct good relations with the rural population (Fall 1967, 275–7). Notwithstanding a major peasant uprising in Nghe–An province in central Vietnam, the Party's 'rectification' campaign was generally successful. By 1958, the countryside was deemed sufficiently pacific for a programme of full-scale collectivization to be launched and, by 1960, eighty-six per cent of the rural population (some 13 million people) were involved in some form of co-operative farming. But because mechanization was virtually non-existent (only 7 per cent of land was ploughed by tractor), agricultural productivity remained low and food shortages continued to be a fact of life (Young 1991, 51; Duiker 1983, 104).

Industrial development was also a priority for the DRV but meant starting almost from scratch. The previously French-owned coal, steel and textile industries were nationalized, but these employed only a few thousand people and had accounted for just 1.5 per cent of North Vietnam's total material output in 1954. For the rest of the decade, the urban economy remained predominantly artisanal and retail, and it was only in 1961 that Hanoi launched a Five Year Plan for the rapid advancement of heavy industry. Helped, however, by economic assistance from China and the Soviet Union to the tune of $1 billion in the 1955–65 period, some progress was being made by the time the Plan neared completion. But from the mid-1960s, as the struggle for the liberation of the south consumed more and more of North Vietnam's manpower and resources, and as the American air war targeted its embryonic industrial infrastructure, nearly all development came to a halt. By most indices, therefore, the DRV remained a poor, industrially underdeveloped, peasant-based society.

The question of how much faith the North Vietnamese put in the 1956 elections ever taking place is one that divides historians. Using communist documentation captured during the 1960s, a number of writers have argued that Hanoi harboured few illusions on this count. This may well have been true, but the North Vietnamese could be forgiven for believing that when the moment arrived, international support for the peace process would ensure that the elections went ahead as planned. Britain, for example, one of the co-chairmen of the Geneva conference, was widely acknowledged as the principal architect of the settlement and could be expected to press for its implementation, whilst the other co-chairman, the Soviet Union, was a fraternal ally of the DRV. When, however, the Saigon government boycotted the elections, Hanoi's indignant protests produced only a muted echo in the international arena. The Soviet Union, under the leadership of Nikita Khrushchev, was beginning to explore the potential for peaceful co-existence with the West and evinced no eagerness to court confrontation with the United States over an issue it considered of limited importance. As for the Chinese, they reacted by demanding the reconvening of the Geneva Conference, but never really pressed the matter. The existing partition arrangement suited China well, providing more than adequate security on its southern frontier, and the Beijing government had scant desire to jeopardize this state of affairs by inviting war with the United States on behalf of North Vietnam, the more so when domestic socialist construction was now its over-riding priority. The British, meanwhile, distanced themselves from the settlement that Anthony Eden, now Prime Minister, had worked so hard to construct. With Vietnam no longer regarded as a potential catalyst for general war (as it had been in 1954), London was disinclined to subject Anglo–American relations to further strain by challenging the Eisenhower administration's interpretation of Geneva.

North Vietnam was thus isolated, disappointed and resentful – but also cautious, ruling out an immediate return to arms as a means of redressing its grievances. Any attempt to extend the Vietnamese revolution to the south in 1956 risked American military retaliation at a time when the revolution in the north was still far from complete, and when its defences were less than impregnable. Hanoi had also to be careful not to antagonize Moscow and Beijing, whose views on the matter had been made clear and on whom it relied for vital military and economic assistance. Accordingly, the Party leadership took the only realistic course open to it and opted to defer, for the time being, the goal of reunification and concentrate instead on completing the north's political, economic and military development. Yet, sensible as this approach was, there were some in the VWP who found it hard to accept, especially those southerners who had moved north in 1954 and, even more so, the Party faithful who had stayed on in the south after partition and who now faced an uncertain future. Ho Chi Minh shared their anxieties, but he also insisted that a tactical retreat was necessary to further the Vietnamese revolution in the future. 'To have a vigorous plant with green leaves, beautiful flowers, and good fruit, we must take good care of it and feed the root', Ho explained. North Vietnam was the root of this plant, the 'root of the struggle for complete national liberation and reunification'. These goals had not been lost sight of, he argued, their attainment was just a matter of timing (Fall 1967, 272–3). As for the method of attainment, North Vietnam's leaders, conscious of the need to court international sympathy, publicly committed themselves to a peaceful solution to the national question. But, privately, they accepted that war might be unavoidable. 'While recognizing the possibility of reunifying Viet-Nam by peaceful means', Ho told the Central Committee in 1956, 'we should always remember that our people's principal enemies are the American imperialists and their agents who still occupy half our country and are preparing for war; therefore, we should firmly hold aloft the banner of peace and enhance our vigilance' (Fall 1967, 270).

The possibility referred to by Ho was really a hope – that the Diem regime's lack of popular support and its questionable legitimacy would lead to its replacement by a more representative government (including the southern communists) with a mandate to resurrect the Geneva settlement and with it the all-Vietnam elections. But Hanoi's hope was also Washington's fear. Between 1955 and 1960 American assistance to South Vietnam – almost $7 billion in total – was instrumental in keeping Diem in power and became, in effect, a substitute for the mass support he was neither willing nor able to cultivate. By the time Eisenhower left office in January 1961, the Republic of Vietnam was the fifth greatest recipient of American foreign aid in the world. Given the obsession of US policy-makers with Cold War concerns, the bulk of this aid went towards enabling Diem to counter the threat of communism. But in providing him with the wherewithal to develop an army (the **ARVN**, or Army of the Republic of Vietnam), a Civil Guard and other security mechanisms, Washington inadvertently gave Diem the means to protect what was, in all key respects, a dictatorship. Instead of the show-case for democracy it had hoped to create in South Vietnam, the United States found itself underwriting a police state.

Looking back, the warning signs had been present from the start in Diem's unashamed élitism, the highly suspicious 98.2 per cent vote in his favour in the 1955 Presidential referendum, and the self-serving RVN constitution of 1956. Thereafter, Diem took matters even further, allocating key positions in his regime to members of his immediate family: his chief adviser, for example, was his younger brother, Ngo Dinh Nhu (who, as Minister of the Interior, also controlled the RVN's notorious secret police and was the most feared man in the country). Throughout the southern Republic, opposition political parties were outlawed, freedom of speech and association greatly restricted, the independence of the press curtailed and criticism of the regime made punishable by detention in concentration camps. Promotion within the government bureaucracy and armed forces depended on loyalty to the Ngo family rather than ability, or on religious denomination before merit, with Catholics the main beneficiaries. Corruption permeated the regime, and it became commonplace for the simplest appeal to the government at any level to be rejected unless accompanied by a financial inducement, or for the ARVN, the civil police and Nhu's *Gestapo* to demand money from innocent people under the threat of charging them as enemies of the state.

Nation building in South Vietnam was also intended to demonstrate to other peasant-dominated societies in Southeast Asia the superiority of the capitalist above the socialist mode of economic development. But the RVN proved to be just as poor an advertisement for the benefits of liberal capitalism as it was for democracy. In the countryside, peasant living standards remained extremely poor, a matter of seeming indifference to the Saigon government which did little to address the problems of excessive rent levels and the unequal distribution of land. Worse, many southern peasants found that land given to them by the Vietminh for nothing before July 1954 was reclaimed by returning landlords in the post-partition period who promptly demanded back-rent. Under American pressure, the Saigon regime did introduce land reform and tenant protection schemes in 1956, but proceeded to turn a blind eye as many landowners circumvented their conditions. For Diem, the idea of cultivating wide rural support was evidently less important than maintaining the political allegiance of the wealthy agrarian capitalists. The result was predictable: the alienation of the largest section of the Vietnamese population. Industrial development was similarly hampered by the government's desire to retain power rather than do anything constructive with it, although the Eisenhower administration's fixation with security hardly helped, with military aid to South Vietnam four times the size of economic and technical assistance. There was, therefore, no economic miracle in South Vietnam, only increasing dependence on American largesse.

Why, it may be asked, did the Eisenhower administration continue to support Diem throughout the second half of the 1950s in the light of his obvious failings? Why were his deficiencies covered up by a costly public relations campaign designed to prove to American and international opinion that nation building was in fact a great success? The answer, many historians tend to agree, is to be found in Diem's one indisputably positive asset – the effectiveness of his anti-communist policies. For, given a choice between an ally who was a good democrat but a poor anti-communist, or a good anti-communist and poor democrat, US Cold War policy-makers invariably opted for the latter. To be sure, the Eisenhower administration repeatedly urged Diem to liberalize and democratize his rule, but as long as Cold War imperatives informed US foreign policy, Washington would never apply the ultimate sanction and withdraw its support.

Diem's anti-communist reputation was built on the success of his method for eliminating 'red' influence in South Vietnam, a process best described as 'dragnetting'. From late 1955, having dealt with his non-communist opponents, Diem turned his full attention to rooting out Vietminh 'stay behinds'. An estimated 5,000–10,000 communist troops had stayed in the south after partition to maintain an underground revolutionary network as insurance against the collapse of the Geneva settlement. From 1954 until he was recalled to Hanoi in 1957, the Regional Committee for the South was under the direction of Le Duan. Although communists and communist-sympathizers were the first targets of the ARVN and Nhu's forces as they systematically scoured the countryside, the trawl was gradually expanded to include anyone, communist or otherwise, considered to be an opponent of the regime. Between 1955 and 1959, some twelve thousand executions took place, with more than fifty thousand people sentenced to re-education in concentration camps (Young 1991, 56). This casual disregard for the fate of the innocent in pursuit of those deemed guilty made 'dragnetting' a highly effective anti-communist device. Research into its impact on one particular district of South Vietnam – the Saigon suburbs of Go Vap and Tan Binh – has shown how communist numbers dropped from a recorded 1,000 in 1954 to 385 in 1957 to a single individual in 1959. By then, there may have been no more than 5,000 VWP members left in the whole of South Vietnam (Young 1991,

64; Duiker 1995, 118). Yet, whatever its merits as an anti-communist tactic, 'dragnetting' did nothing for the popularity of the Saigon government amongst an already disaffected peasant population. Indeed it probably accelerated the alienation of its theoretical rural constituency, ensuring the active support of many and the benevolent neutrality of many more for any movement that could mount a challenge to Saigon's violent impositions. Nor was discontent confined to the rural population: in the towns and cities, too, there was mounting unhappiness with Diem's repressive and authoritarian rule amongst the educated, professional and intellectual classes, whilst the Buddhists, and the Cao Dai and Hoa Hao, were united in condemnation of the Catholic bias of his government.

When the Diemist terror first began, the southern communists had looked north for support only to be told by Hanoi to stay underground, concentrate on organizing popular protest against the cancellation of all-Vietnam elections, and react to Saigon aggression solely in self-defence. In offering this advice, the DRV leadership was clearly anxious to avoid any action that the United States might interpret as external aggression and use as justification for large-scale armed intervention in defence of the southern state. Militarily, the DRV was still far from ready to oversee the forced liberation of the south, never mind contemplate possible war with a superpower. Therefore, to the dismay of the Regional Committee for the South, Hanoi continued to place the political, economic and military consolidation of the revolution in the north before the liberation of the south. This estimate of priorities held good for nearly three years, but by the start of 1959, a combination of pressures forced the VWP leadership to rethink its position. First, the mounting unpopularity of the Diem regime had created tremendous revolutionary potential in South Vietnam. Second, if the Diemist terror continued unchecked, there would be few communists left in the south to convert this potential into revolutionary action. It was against this backdrop that, in January 1959, the Fifteenth Plenum of the VWP Central Committee took what Party historians later termed the 'milestone' decision to adopt a more activist approach in the south. This is not to say that North Vietnam committed itself to a policy of all-out armed struggle, but it did mark a turning point in the Vietnamese revolution, the moment when the defence of the north and the liberation of the south assumed a roughly equal status.

Over the next eighteen months, Hanoi approved various measures designed to increase the pressure on the Diem regime. These included a recruitment drive in the south to offset losses incurred since 1954; allowing southern political cadres to take the lead in organizing political opposition to Diem; infiltrating some 4,000 southern-born communists back into South Vietnam via a network of paths in Laos and Cambodia that would later develop into the Ho Chi Minh trail; the funnelling of supplies and military hardware to the south by the same route, and the sanctioning of a higher though still restricted level of revolutionary violence. Although these measures constituted a definite escalation in North Vietnam's commitment, they fell some way short of explicit sanction for all-out war in the south, and evidence suggests that the dual spectre of American intervention and Sino–Soviet disapproval continued to loom large in Hanoi's thinking. The southern Party leaders, on the other hand, seem to have taken the DRV's new line as implicit approval for a major politico-military insurgency against the Diem regime. This, at any rate, is what their actions in South Vietnam added up to in 1959 and 1960. Communist-led peasant uprisings resulted in the 'liberation' of large areas of the countryside from Saigon control, the introduction of extensive land reform measures and the organization of the local population into self-defence units to protect their newly acquired freedoms. ARVN forces sent to restore order were frequently attacked and defeated, their US-supplied weapons passing into communist hands. At the same time, assassinations and abductions of Saigon government officials became widespread, and assaults on government buildings and installations increased.

Was this upsurge in violence the *intended* outcome of North Vietnam's decision to accord the liberation of the south heightened importance? Or was it a case of the southern communists, after years of repression, finding it hard to contain their desire for retribution and adopting a level of aggression that Hanoi found unacceptable but difficult to restrain? There are no clear answers to these questions, but together they form the heart of the historical debate over the origins of the second Vietnam war – or, it might be argued, the resumption of the original conflict after a six-year stand-off. In September 1960, the Third VWP Congress in Hanoi voted to support a policy of armed struggle in the south, a decision which, at first sight, seems to validate the proposition that North Vietnam was leading from the front. Yet, while undoubtedly a decision of great significance, it may have been more a case of Hanoi acknowledging a *fait accompli* by the southern revolutionary forces – the armed struggle having begun, it could hardly be disowned, as the southern leaders probably knew. It could also be argued that in committing itself fully to the struggle in the south, North Vietnam could expect to exert a control over events, and an influence on revolutionary strategy, that had been conspicuously lacking during the previous two years.

In fact, controlling and even containing the insurgency is the most striking feature of the Party leadership's actions in the wake of the 1960 Congress. Rather than a general call to arms, Hanoi urged the creation of a broad-based *political* movement as the principal vehicle of revolution in South Vietnam, an amalgam of all shades of anti-Diemist opinion. As with the earlier Vietminh, in order to avoid narrowing the base of the movement through the estrangement of non-communist nationalists, the leading role of the southern communists was to be obscured. Therefore, whilst the use of armed force was obviously necessary in any confrontation with Diemist militarism, it is clear that this consideration did not predominate in Hanoi's calculations, rather, a combined politico-military strategy was seen as the key to success. Success itself was defined as the removal of the Diem regime and its replacement by a more representative government in which the southern communists would exercise a dominating, if necessarily disguised, influence. The new Saigon government would then terminate the American military-advisory presence and move towards reunification with the north. Importantly, such a politico-military strategy – unlike all-out war – was thought to minimize the risk of a major US military response. Interestingly, the decision of the Third Party Congress to approve a Five Year Plan for the extensive industrial development of the north, not to mention major on-going efforts to collectivize the agricultural sector, indicates a certain optimism that objectives in the south could be attained short of major warfare, and certainly without provoking damaging US military retaliation above the 17th parallel.

Encouraged by Hanoi, in December 1960 southern cadres took the lead in founding the National Liberation Front for South Vietnam (NLF). The NLF was an umbrella grouping encompassing a wide variety of nationalist/anti-RVN opinion. Peasants, workers, intellectuals, members of the professions and religious sects, representatives from ethnic minorities and Buddhists were all to be found within its ranks. But, like the Vietminh before it, the handle of the umbrella was in the firm – if disguised – grip of the communists. By early 1962, the

People's Revolutionary Party (**PRP**) had emerged as the dominant force within the NLF's Central Committee: in spite of the absence of any obvious links with North Vietnam, the PRP is now regarded as the effective southern branch of the VWP, controlled by and answerable to Hanoi. The NLF's programme, first revealed in January 1961, deliberately avoided communist slogans and instead stressed patriotic-nationalist goals, democratic freedoms, anti-colonialism, anti-Americanism, land reform, fairer wages, promotion of domestic industry over foreign imports, a neutral foreign policy and peaceful reunification with the north.

As already noted, it was vital from Hanoi's standpoint that the NLF should be seen to be southern-indigenous in composition so that the campaign against Diem, regardless of the level of North Vietnam's direction and material input, would possess the essential characteristics of a civil war. But of equal importance was the need to ensure that communist influence (southern or northern) was hidden so that the struggle bore a nationalist rather than ideological or Cold War imprimatur. This approach was determined by the need to avoid antagonizing the United States, both as an end in itself and in order to retain the good offices of Moscow and Beijing, neither of whom wished to see the insurgency escalate into a potentially incendiary Cold War conflict by proxy as the Franco–Vietminh war had in 1954. Yet, for all the efforts at concealment, there was never any doubt in the minds of US policymakers that the NLF was a communist 'front' organization under the overall control of North Vietnam, and that behind North Vietnam lay the shadow of Communist China and the Soviet Union. The repeated assertions of Hanoi and the NLF that the insurgency was a spontaneous and independent reaction in the south against the Diem regime and the American presence did nothing to dent this conviction. Historical opinion, on the other hand, was for a long time divided between those who shared the US government's view and those who, like the American anti-war movement in the 1960s, accepted Vietnamese communist claims at face value. Now, however, it appears that the official Washington appreciation was the correct one – indeed evidence emanating from Hanoi itself in the 1980s and 1990s has confirmed this. Whatever the truth about the extent of North Vietnam's role in the period leading up to the outbreak of the insurgency, there is little doubt that the NLF was, in the words of a leading authority on the communist side of the war, 'an insurgent movement inspired by local conditions in the south but guided and directed from Hanoi' (Duiker 1995, 137).

During 1961, political opposition to the Diem regime began to coalesce around the NLF, while its military wing – the People's Liberation Armed Force (**PLAF**) or Vietcong – developed into an increasingly effective fighting force. By the autumn, official American estimates placed Vietcong strength in the region of 16,000 and 'voluntary, positive support' for the insurgency possibly as high as 200,000, or 2 per cent of the population. Around 4,500 southern-born communists had been infiltrated into the south, and into the ranks of the Vietcong, by the end of 1960 (*FRUS 1961-63*, I, 484–6; Hunt 1996, 35). Organizationally, the military effort was directed by the Central Office of South Vietnam (**COSVN**), a Field Headquarters answerable to Hanoi. Structurally, the Vietcong was a three-tiered force: at the bottom were local self-defence units, farmers by day, guerrillas by night; above them were large regional guerrilla units, on permanent call; and finally main force units, built out of the best elements in the regionals, organized into regular military formations, and under direct COSVN command. As with the Vietminh army in 1946–54, the Vietcong planned a military campaign in three stages – an initial guerrilla war, to be followed by a move to larger conventional offensives, and finally a general offensive aimed at engineering the overthrow of the Saigon government. Parallel to the unfolding of military strategy, the NLF's political activities were designed to create the conditions for a popular uprising to accompany the general military offensive. The Front, like the Vietcong armed forces, was constructed as a pyramid. At the top was the Central Committee, or Presidium. Then came provincial, district and local echelons, administered by political cadres. And at the base were mass organizations, established to attract support from all progressive elements in society. These organizations were the most visible manifestation of the NLF at the 'rice roots' level. Some were based on occupation (peasants, workers, writers, artists or students), while others aimed at attracting religious or ethnic groups (Buddhists, Catholics, members of national minorities). The largest grouping was, predictably, the Farmer's Liberation Association, with nearly 2 million members by 1963.

From the outset, it was clear that the success of the NLF/Vietcong's politico-military strategy – in essence a revival of the Maoist-inspired 'Peoples' War' approach used by the Vietminh – hinged on keeping the United States out of the conflict, and that this in turn depended on carefully controlling the level of insurgent success. Too much could provoke serious US intervention, but just enough might give rise to fears in Washington of a protracted and costly commitment and lead either to disengagement or a negotiated settlement on NLF/Vietcong terms. 'How far we win, how far they lose', Le Duan observed, 'must be calculated and measured precisely' (Duiker 1995, 155). But as events would show, for all Hanoi's calculations and measurements, there was to be no avoiding a show-down with the United States.

CHAPTER FOUR

Insurgency and counter-insurgency: the struggle for South Vietnam, 1961–5

Just as the communist-led insurgency in South Vietnam was beginning to take shape, a new United States administration came to power in Washington under the Democrat President John F. Kennedy. Kennedy had long been interested in Vietnam and believed that the preservation of a separate non-communist state in the south was a 'test of American responsibility and determination in Asia' (Young 1991, 58). In addition, Kennedy had argued during his election campaign that the Republicans had failed to deter communist revolutionary movements in the Third World, a claim that, on its own, would have rendered South Vietnam a test of whether the Democrats could do any better. On the eve of Kennedy's inauguration, however, the Soviet leader Khrushchev raised the stakes when, in a much-publicized speech, he declared his country's support for wars of national liberation in the Third World. The Kennedy administration duly determined to meet the challenge implicit in Khrushchev's pronouncement by defeating the NLF/Vietcong in South Vietnam. In this way, the United States would send a clear message to potential insurgents elsewhere – and to Moscow and Beijing – that wars of national liberation could not succeed, and that Western interests in the Third World would be fiercely defended.

It took the Kennedy administration some months to decide on the means to this end, months during which greater Cold War problems (particularly Cuba and Berlin) demanded immediate action. Also competing for Washington's attention at this time was Vietnam's Indochinese neighbour, Laos, where a civil war had erupted between the US-backed government in Vientiane and the communist-led Pathet

Lao, supported by North Vietnam and the Soviet Union. So serious was the situation that the Eisenhower administration, in its final days, even considered military intervention on behalf of the beleaguered anti-communist forces. Kennedy, however, rejected the military option in favour of a negotiated solution. An internationally-sponsored conference opened in Geneva in May 1961, attended by representatives of all concerned Laotian parties, and in July 1962 a settlement was reached whereby a government of national unity would be formed (including both the Pathet Lao and non-communist elements) that would commit itself to a position of neutrality in the Cold War. Nineteen countries, including America, the Soviet Union and China, agreed to respect the agreement. The question of why Kennedy was prepared to accept a negotiated solution for Laos but not for Vietnam has naturally exercised historians over the years. The key difference seems to have been that in South Vietnam, the United States was defending an existing and already considerable commitment, whereas in Laos the investment was far less and the room to man-oeuvre consequently far greater. Moreover, if Laos was genuinely neutralized, it would allow the United States to focus all its attention on the issue in South Vietnam instead of dissipating it throughout Indochina.

The Kennedy administration's investigation of the problem in Vietnam climaxed in November 1961 in a redefinition of its nature. Under Eisenhower, the South Vietnamese army had been primed to meet a conventional main-force invasion from North Vietnam, with southern-based guerrilla activity dismissed as a weakening pre-liminary. But to Kennedy and his advisers, it now looked like the ARVN had been trained to fight the wrong war against the wrong enemy, for as the insurgency gathered pace, it began to resemble the main event itself. Acting on this conclusion, Kennedy ordered a substantial increase in the number of US advisers to the South Vietnamese military, their brief to educate select ARVN units in *counter*-insurgency. In doing so, the President resisted pressure from several sources (notably his top military advisers) for a more drastic form of escalation, including the deployment of US combat forces. Kennedy did, however, approve a secret CIA effort in Laos to disrupt the Ho Chi Minh trail, the despatch of South Vietnamese commando units to the north on covert sabotage missions, and the continuation of the Eisenhower policy of large-scale economic and military assistance to Saigon combined with exhortations to Diem to liberalize his rule. Diem, as ever, accepted the aid but not the advice.

When Eisenhower had left office, there were 875 US military personnel in South Vietnam. At the end of 1963, such was the level of the Kennedy administration's commitment, the number had risen to 16,263. During the same period, American aid averaged $400 million per annum, the overall strength of South Vietnam's armed forces increased from 243,000 to 514,000 men, and a co-ordinating body, the US Military Assistance Command, Vietnam (**MACV**), was established in Saigon (Lewy 1978, 24, 455). Principal responsibility for training the ARVN in counter-insurgency fell to the US Army Special Forces Group (the Green Berets). Inevitably, US instructors indulged in education-through-demonstration, taking an active though unacknowledged part in operations designed to deal with the insurgents at the village level. The United States also bolstered the ARVN with state-of-the-art military technology; helicopter gunships, for example, provided tremendous mobility and firepower as well as a means of dispensing herbicides and defoliants to poison food crops and destroy the jungle cover in Vietcong-dominated areas. But as well as taking the war to the enemy, American policy extended to efforts to cut the enemy off from the rural population. Working on the assumption that peasant support for the insurgency was the product not of consent but of Vietcong terror, a joint US–RVN Strategic Hamlet Programme was launched in the spring of 1962. The Programme involved shepherding millions of people into purpose-built fortified hamlets where they would be safe from Vietcong intimidation. The peasants would continue their normal agrarian labours but, in addition, social welfare initiatives (including the building of schools and health centres inside the hamlets) would be launched in an effort to foster loyalty towards the Saigon government. Denied access to its primary source of recruitment, revenue, food and sanctuary, the Vietcong was expected to attack the hamlets in large numbers, enabling the 'new' ARVN to register a series of telling blows.

Such was the theory. In practice, it was a rather different story. To begin with, the key premise underpinning the scheme was badly flawed: peasant support for the insurgency was often *willingly* given, partly because of the appeal of the NLF's manifesto and the perception of the Vietcong as the lineal descendant of the revered Vietminh, and partly because of fear and hatred of the Saigon government. But the manner in which the Programme was administered also contributed to its undoing. When rural communities displayed little enthusiasm for the initiative, Saigon's agents employed the crudest persuasion methods. Once inside the hamlets, many peasants found they had to build and pay for their new homes in spite of the fact that the construction materials had been donated free by the United States, or that the economic aid intended to enhance their quality of life (again supplied gratis by the Americans) had been siphoned off by corrupt administrators. The barbed wire, high fences and moats surrounding the hamlets created the by no means erroneous impression that the Diem government, in the name of combating the insurgency, really sought to exercise control over the largest and most restive section of the population. But hamlet security (whether in terms of keeping the Vietcong out or the peasants in) was seriously deficient. Over time, night-duty and sometimes full defence responsibility was transferred to specially created hamlet militias, but because they often contained rebel sympathizers, the Vietcong experienced little difficulty in penetrating or destroying many of the hamlets.

Looking back, it is plain that by the spring of 1963, the majority of the 3,225 hamlets the South Vietnamese government claimed to have built were no longer functioning. The Vietcong, meanwhile, was openly levying taxes in 42 of the RVN's 44 provinces, proof that its primacy in the countryside had not diminished. Politically, the NLF now had 300,000 members, with a general following of more than a million (Duiker 1995, 158; 1996, 232). At the time, however, the extent of insurgent success was not so obvious. On the contrary, Saigon authorities, on whom the Americans relied for progress reports, proclaimed the Hamlet Programme a great success, insisting that one-third of the population (around 4 million people) were effectively quarantined. The desire of the South Vietnamese to keep their benefactors happy – to tell the Americans what they wanted to hear – evidently triumphed over their belief in statistical accuracy, and US Defence Secretary Robert McNamara later acknowledged that he and others in Washington received a badly 'distorted' picture from Saigon during 1962 and 1963 (Chomsky 1993, 71). In retrospect, not just the Strategic Hamlets but the whole counter-insurgency effort was unravelling. Even in the first large-scale conventional engagement of the conflict, in January 1963 at Ap Bac in the Mekong delta, the ARVN was still unable to get the better of the Vietcong despite the advantage of numerical and technological superiority.

Yet, in spite of Ap Bac, the Kennedy administration continued to believe that progress was being made, McNamara declaring in April 1963 that '...every quantitative measurement we have shows we are winning this war' (Hunt 1996, 62). Nevertheless, doubts persisted in Washington as to whether a final conclusive victory could ever be secured while Diem remained in power in Saigon. His contempt for democracy, his nepotism, and his readiness to countenance official corruption all seemed to be pushing non-communist Vietnamese into the NLF/Vietcong orbit. It was, however, a combination of developments in the spring and summer of 1963 that finally convinced Kennedy and a majority of his senior Vietnam strategists that a change of government had become essential. The first was Diem's excessively violent reaction to Buddhist demonstrations against the Catholic bias of his regime. As the protests grew in size and regularity, becoming a focus for many shades of anti-government opinion, Diem responded by sending in the army. But far from restoring order, his action only triggered a cycle of violence, with greater unrest leading to harsher repression. International opinion was outraged by the brutality of Diem's methods, and in Washington an embarrassed Kennedy administration came under pressure to justify its support for the Saigon government. The second development concerned rumours that Diem's brother, Nhu, was actively exploring the possibility of a rapprochement with North Vietnam. If, as evidence suggests, there was indeed a degree of north–south dialogue in 1963, what could have prompted Nhu to take such a step? One explanation is that as a committed nationalist, he may have sensed that the longer the insurgency went on the greater the danger of large-scale American intervention and a concomitant erosion of South Vietnam's autonomy, a concern undoubtedly shared by Diem. But he may also have foreseen a more disturbing consequence of American escalation, namely the physical destruction of much of Vietnam in pursuit of Washington's Cold War objectives. Despite the ideological gulf separating their respective governments, the people of the DRV and the RVN were all Vietnamese and, in this most basic link, Nhu and others perhaps discerned the basis of a political solution encompassing the ejection of all US personnel from South Vietnam, its Cold War neutralization and a *modus vivendi* with the north. But to the Kennedy administration, neutralization, whilst tolerable in Laos, was considered too risky in South Vietnam where there was far more to lose when, as most US policy-makers agreed, it led to the eventual communization of the country. Whatever the truth of the matter, these rumours, together with the Saigon government's over-reaction to the Buddhist unrest, were more than sufficient to convince many in Washington that Diem had to go.

American intelligence sources in Saigon had been aware for some time that a number of high-ranking ARVN officers, unhappy with Diem's conduct of the war, his arbitrary promotions policy and the Buddhist repression (the army contained a high proportion of Buddhists) were contemplating a coup. The plotters were reluctant to act, however, without an assurance of American support. The extent to which the Kennedy administration provided this guarantee – and was, therefore, complicit in the coup – has long been a matter of speculation, but it now seems clear that CIA agents informed the rebel Generals that the United States was committed to the Republic of Vietnam, not to any one leader, and that this most subtle of green lights had the approval of the White House. A last appeal to Diem from the American Ambassador in Saigon to accept the need for reform came to nothing and, on the night of 1 November 1963, the Generals made their move. By the morning, both Diem and Nhu were dead and a Military Revolutionary Council installed in their stead. On 7 November, the United States recognized the new government which, for its part, pledged to wage the war to a successful conclusion. It would, however, be left to a new American President to preside over Vietnam policy in the post-Diem period for, on 22 November 1963, Kennedy was himself assassinated in Dallas, Texas.

In spite of the change of government in Saigon, the RVN's military and political fortunes deteriorated to such an extent that, by the spring of 1965, the NLF/Vietcong appeared to be on the brink of complete victory. In Washington, Kennedy's successor as President, Lyndon B. Johnson, reacted to this danger by ordering an enormous increase in the US military commitment, including the widespread aerial bombing of North Vietnam and the despatch of more than half a million combat troops to South Vietnam. Instead of producing victory, however, this escalation resulted in American entrapment, appalling casualty figures on all sides and the devastation of much of Vietnam. It also led many Americans to conclude that the conflict was 'Johnson's war', that the horror was in some way the sole responsibility of the President. It was a characterization Johnson himself deplored. 'This is America's war', he insisted in October 1967. 'If I drop dead tomorrow, this war will still be with you' (Berman 1989, i). Nevertheless, the perception took root and, later, assumed more disquieting form in the writings of former Kennedy associates like Arthur Schlesinger Jnr, Pierre Salinger and Kenneth O'Donnell who all argued that Kennedy, at the time of his death, had decided that South Vietnam could not be saved and was on the verge of terminating the US commitment. The ensuing escalation under Johnson was, therefore, a betrayal of the Kennedy legacy.

Is the withdrawal thesis merely wishful thinking on the part of those Americans who want to believe that Vietnam was an avoidable disaster, or does it rest on firm evidential foundations? According to US government sources, in the summer of 1962 Kennedy instructed McNamara to begin investigation of disengagement options. The process culminated in October 1963 with Kennedy's approval of National Security Action Memorandum #263 (NSAM-263) which recommended 'implementation of plans to withdraw 1,000 US military personnel by the end of 1963' (FRUS 1961–1963, IV, 395–6). Kennedy died the following month and instead of gradual disengagement the United States embarked on gradual escalation. Adherents of the withdrawal thesis contend that Johnson, a domestic politician naive in the ways of international affairs, was either manipulated by bellicose military advisers into accepting a more warlike policy or, alternatively, that his aggressive personality led him willingly to embrace a more offensive approach. In contrast, opponents of the thesis argue that it is based on a deliberate misreading of the evidence and that an objective analysis leads to a wholly different conclusion, namely that Kennedy would have battled on in Vietnam. In endorsing NSAM-263, Kennedy was actually approving – to quote directly from the document – 'Section I B (1–3)' of a report drawn up by McNamara and General Maxwell Taylor, chairman of the Joint Chiefs of Staff. The relevant section of this report stated that the projected withdrawal was to be announced 'in low key as an initial step in a long-term program to replace US personnel with trained Vietnamese without impairment of the war effort' (FRUS 1961–1963, IV, 395–6, 336–46). The latter caveat is critical. Withdrawal plans were clearly conditional on prior success, and success meant either total victory against the insurgents or, at a minimum, proof that the South Vietnamese government could cope with the insurgency on its own. Johnson went on to abandon NSAM-263 because it was only in the weeks following Diem's overthrow that an accurate assessment of the situation finally emerged – one that revealed NLF/Vietcong strength, Saigon politico-military weakness, and hence the total absence of the indispensable prerequisite for withdrawal. This was the reality Johnson faced. It was also the reality Kennedy would have faced had he lived.

On balance, the case for unconditional withdrawal is not wholly convincing. It rests on a questionable interpretation of the documentary record and hearsay testimony from a number of former Kennedy aides who, in exonerating Kennedy from any part in the later disaster in Vietnam, effectively exonerate themselves. Whether Kennedy would have adopted the same escalatory measures as Johnson, taken them to such extremes or persisted with them for so long is, of course, another question. The least that may be said is that Kennedy would have found it just as difficult as Johnson to simply walk away from the problem. Perhaps, therefore, the real irony is that those who subscribe to the withdrawal thesis might do better to mourn the passing of Diem and Nhu rather than Kennedy.

Whatever Kennedy might or might not have done, Johnson's early decisions were taken in the belief that he was following at least the general policy lines of his predecessor. Thus, within forty-eight hours of taking office, he had announced that the US commitment to South Vietnam remained undiminished and, in private, expressed his desire to 'win the war' (*FRUS 1961–1963*, IV, 636). NSAM-273, authorized by Johnson on 26 November 1963, formally superseded NSAM-263 and the withdrawal option. The new Presidential directive attested that the 'central object' of US policy was to help the government and people of the Republic of Vietnam 'to win their contest against the externally directed and supported communist conspiracy'. Disengagement remained a future objective, but it was conditional, as NSAM-263 had always insisted, on prior success (*FRUS 1961–1963*, IV, 596, 395–6, 638).

The problem for the Johnson administration was how to achieve that success. Initially, the new President resisted pressure from the Joint Chiefs of Staff for a serious expansion in the US effort, including air attacks against North Vietnam and aerial interdiction of the burgeoning Ho Chi Minh trail in Laos. Instead, Johnson approved a modest increase in American advisers to South Vietnam in the hope that a revitalized counter-insurgency strategy, together with the advent of a regime in Saigon determined to prosecute the war with vigour, would stem the tide of insurgent success. Johnson also authorized further covert operations against North Vietnam, including intelligence-gathering and pinprick attacks along the coast by RVN commando units. But still the news remained bleak, US military intelligence reporting in March 1964 that the communists controlled between forty and forty-five per cent of the South Vietnamese countryside (along with fifty per cent of the population), and that the Strategic Hamlet Programme was on the verge of disintegration (Duiker 1995, 165). At the same time, Vietcong attacks on Saigon forces had intensified, leading to lowered ARVN morale and heightened desertion levels, whilst NLF political initiatives were contributing to mounting worker and student unrest in many large cities. In Saigon, the ruling military junta had succumbed to factionalism and in-fighting, a development that did little to advance the war effort, never mind promote political stability or social and democratic reform. Moreover, this already serious situation was, from the American and South Vietnamese viewpoint, about to worsen still further.

In December 1963, the VWP Central Committee in Hanoi had passed a resolution supporting a dramatic escalation in the insurgency. The objective was to destroy the ARVN and eliminate the remaining Strategic Hamlets in preparation for the launch of the long-planned general offensive and popular uprising. Thereafter, two possibilities would open up. The first was the complete collapse of the Saigon regime and its replacement by a new coalition dominated by the NLF, one that would terminate the US presence, promote a neutral solution for South Vietnam and, in due course, reunite with the north. The second and more straightforward possibility was an outright NLF/Vietcong victory. As a first step, there was to be an expansion in the numbers and fighting quality of the Vietcong through a recruitment drive in the south and greater infiltration of arms and supplies via the Ho Chi Minh trail. On the political front, the NLF was to broaden still further its popular base whilst, within the NLF itself, the southern communists were to extend their hidden-hand influence.

Le Duan, VWP General Secretary since 1960, later recalled that the resolution was only passed after heated debate between those who feared American retaliation against the north (via bombing, invasion or both) and so counselled caution, and a more militant faction – led by Le Duan himself – that believed the situation in the south demanded escalation. With Ho Chi Minh in failing health, Le Duan had begun to exercise an increasing dominance over Party decision-making, arguing on this occasion that the removal of Diem was a mixed blessing, for it had been the excesses of his rule that had helped create the revolutionary opportunity in the south in the first place. If the new Saigon leadership confounded expectations and introduced a meaningful reformist political programme attractive to moderates in the NLF, the revolutionary momentum could be lost. Of equal concern was increased American participation in the defence of South Vietnam even if the insurgency remained at current levels. In accepting Le Duan's arguments and in agreeing to step-up the insurgency, therefore, Party leaders sought to pre-empt this dual threat to the completion of the Vietnamese revolution.

Because of the resolution on escalation, the Central Committee's 1963 Plenum has come to be seen as one of the most important in VWP history. But some historians have invested it with added significance, seeing it as the point when the restraint that had hitherto characterized Hanoi's thinking was abandoned and a decision taken to commit units of the regular North Vietnamese Army (the People's Army of Vietnam, PAVN) to fight in the south. It now appears that between five and six thousand North Vietnamese troops were infiltrated into the RVN in 1964–5 and that the most senior North Vietnamese commander next to Giap, General Nguyen Chi Thanh, was appointed to head the COSVN and oversee the expansion of the war (Lomperis 1984, 64; Lewy 1978, 40). But it is less certain that this had been the intention in December 1963. It may have been that the continuing fragmentation of the RVN during the first half of 1964 encouraged Hanoi to go for broke. The risk of inviting American counter-escalation was obvious, but it was evidently outweighed by the prospect of delivering a final crushing blow to the South Vietnamese government and armed forces and ensuring, in the process, that there was little left for the United States to intervene to defend. Confronted with a hopeless situation, the Johnson administration would cut its losses and withdraw. If this was indeed Hanoi's reasoning, it was to prove a serious miscalculation.

Even before the impact of Hanoi's decision to escalate was felt in South Vietnam, a military consensus had formed in Washington in favour of firm US action. A consensus, moreover, that perceived the source of the problem to be North Vietnam's material assistance for, and political direction of, the insurgency, and a consensus that saw the solution in an aerial bombing campaign against the DRV. The bombing would be undertaken on a graduated basis, the intensity increasing incrementally. There would, however, be regular pauses during which Hanoi would be given the chance to negotiate an end to the destruction of its precious industrial base in return for an end to its support for the insurgency. If North Vietnam failed to conform to what one historian has termed the 'logic of the rack', the bombing would be resumed at a greater level of destruction before the next pause was introduced (Young 1991, 113). Should the air campaign fail in its primary objective, the US military expected it to so disrupt North Vietnam's capacity to send men and war materiel down the Ho Chi Minh trail that the threat posed by the insurgent forces would be reduced to more manageable proportions.

By the spring of 1964, the Joint Chiefs of Staff had drawn up bombing plans that targeted North Vietnam's petroleum, oil and lubricants storage areas, industrial complexes and lines of communication. Yet Johnson, despite the seriousness of the situation, refused to authorize their implementation. The reason, he later explained, was his desire 'to seek the fullest support of Congress for any major action that I took' (Johnson 1971, 115). A draft resolution had been drawn up alongside the bombing plans, but Johnson saw little hope of Congressional approval. Existing evidence of North Vietnam's 'aggression' against South Vietnam was probably insufficient to win the support of liberal Democrats for warlike action, and few Republicans were likely to help Johnson look *tough* on communism when, in a Presidential election year, their campaign was stressing the opposite – that he was *weak* on communism, especially in Asia. Bombing plans were thus on hold when, at the start of August 1964, an incident off the coast of North Vietnam led, in rapid time, to the removal of all Congressional constraints on Johnson's Vietnam policy.

On 2 August, North Vietnamese torpedo boats attacked a US destroyer on patrol in the Gulf of Tonkin. A second destroyer was despatched to the area in a support role. On 4 August, both were allegedly attacked by North Vietnamese gunboats and duly returned fire. President Johnson ordered immediate air strikes against DRV naval installations in retaliation for what he claimed was 'open aggression on the high seas'. He then asked for, and on 7 August was given, Congressional approval to act in similar fashion if or when the need arose. The Gulf of Tonkin resolution, passed virtually unanimously in Congress, would provide the legal basis for the subsequent air war against North Vietnam and the commitment of US ground troops to the defence of South Vietnam. Given these far-reaching repercussions, it is no surprise that historians have subjected the episode to particular scrutiny. One of the main lines of inquiry has focused on whether Congress, in supporting the resolution, effectively surrendered its Constitutional right to declare war, at least in the Southeast Asian context. Whether, that is, Congress provided the

President with a 'blank cheque' to frame and execute Vietnam policy as only he and his closest advisers saw fit. On the face of it, the answer is yes. Congress, the resolution stated, 'supports the determination of the President, as Commander-in-Chief, to take all necessary measures to repel any armed attack against the forces of the United States and to prevent further aggression'. The resolution also empowered Johnson to take 'all necessary measures, including the use of armed force', to protect SEATO members and, crucially, SEATO protocol states like the Republic of Vietnam. In short, the President was given advance sanction to bomb North Vietnam and defend South Vietnam with US forces if, in *his* judgement, such action was deemed necessary (Commager 1968, 714).

In fairness to Congress, it later emerged that administration spokesmen had been economical with the truth when providing details of what took place in the Gulf. Far from being an unprovoked attack, the North Vietnamese action was probably in retaliation for covert US monitoring of their radar capacity, and US support for South Vietnamese commando raids along their coastline. Furthermore, few if any of those that voted for it in August 1964 ever envisaged the resolution underwriting the kind of escalation that took place in Vietnam between 1965 and 1968, and when that was exactly what it did do, many on Capitol Hill believed they had been manipulated, even lied to by Johnson and his associates. As for the North Vietnamese, all the signs are that until August 1964 they believed that the United States, when faced with the prospect of a costly war on behalf of a weak and deeply unpopular government in Saigon, would opt to disengage, perhaps negotiating a settlement on the lines of Laos in 1962. However, the firmness of Johnson's response to the Gulf of Tonkin incident, together with the import of the follow-up resolution, caused strategists in Hanoi to revise this estimate. In fact, it was probably at this point, rather than December 1963, that the decision was taken to send regular units of the North Vietnamese army to the south in an effort to hasten the collapse of the Saigon government before the Americans had the chance to act on the Gulf of Tonkin resolution and intervene in force. Certainly, by the end of 1964, three North Vietnamese regiments (some 4,500 men) were in place in the south (Lewy 1978, 39–40). Critics of the Johnson administration would later charge that any escalation in North Vietnamese involvement in South Vietnam was triggered by prior American escalation, in particular the intensive bombing of the DRV that began in March 1965. Despite US government efforts to argue otherwise, opponents of the war persisted with the claim. However, it was clearly North Vietnam that made the first important major escalatory move, and today, after decades of denying that its troops were ever involved in South Vietnam, Hanoi has dropped the pretence and now freely admits that its full resources were brought to bear in defeating the United States and its RVN ally (Duiker 1996, 3).

It has often been said of Lyndon Johnson that he was determined from the very outset of his Presidency on an expanded US commitment in South Vietnam as part of an aggressive Containment policy in Southeast Asia. As such, the Gulf of Tonkin resolution was just a staging post on a straight and pre-determined road to the Americanization of the war. In recent years, however, this orthodoxy has been challenged. For example, if escalation was always his goal, why did Johnson continue to resist pressure from his Service Chiefs to bomb North Vietnam even after passage of the Gulf of Tonkin resolution gave him the authority to do so, and even though the situation in South Vietnam appeared to demand it? An obvious answer is that Johnson was never going to do anything dramatic before the November 1964 Presidential election. Yet Johnson continued to stay his hand *after* his landslide electoral victory over the Republican, Barry Goldwater. The reason, according to fresh research, is that he was far more hesitant about escalation than was previously thought, and was deeply troubled about the repercussions of greater involvement in what he called 'the biggest damn mess I ever saw' (*New York Times*, 1997). Unlike the self-explanatory orthodox view of Johnson as a 'bloodthirsty hawk', this more nuanced interpretation requires elaboration (Divine 1988, 91).

By the autumn of 1964, the consensus within the US government in favour of launching an air war against North Vietnam had broadened considerably. But when Johnson sought a firm assurance that bombing would make a decisive contribution to the resolution of the problem, his top advisers were – understandably – unable to provide one. Uncertainty about the positive benefits of escalation gave Johnson pause for thought, but so did the possibility that air strikes might have worryingly negative consequences. However much the Joint Chiefs of Staff played down the risk, Chinese intervention in support of North Vietnam could not be ruled out and, with it, a wider war with all its related dangers. The reaction of the Soviet Union was also difficult to predict following Khrushchev's replacement in October 1964 by a new hard-line leadership. Furthermore, Johnson was informed by his experts that North Vietnam and the Vietcong could well react to American bombing by launching an all-out effort to destroy the Republic of Vietnam. Given the chronic weakness of the Saigon regime, the communists might succeed unless the United States was prepared to contemplate a serious ground force commitment. Johnson, however, had hoped that air action against North Vietnam would obviate the need for large-scale American troop deployments, the thought of which, he confessed, 'makes the chills run up my back' (*New York Times*, 1997). But now, as 1965 dawned, it appeared that bombing North Vietnam might actually make a troop deployment inevitable. Accordingly, Johnson insisted on the establishment of stability in the south – on demonstrable proof that the Saigon government could withstand whatever the communists threw at it by way of retaliation – as an essential pre-requisite to escalation against the north.

Far from the hawk of legend, therefore, Johnson emerges from this revised assessment as a brake on the Joint Chiefs of Staff and others who favoured extreme action. In the face of the consensus in favour of the use of air power in some form, Johnson temporized – and continued to do so in spite of a series of communist attacks on US bases and personnel in late 1964 sufficiently damaging to warrant a major riposte. These incidents occurred at a time of mounting communist success and corresponding RVN reverses, and prompted Ambassador Maxwell Taylor in Saigon to warn Johnson in December that for the United States to take 'no positive action now is to accept defeat in the fairly near future'. Taylor's sombre judgement was echoed in Washington by the Joint Chiefs of Staff, McNamara and other influential figures in the administration (Herring 1986, 128). Johnson did take positive action – but not the kind his advisers had in mind – by agreeing to the secret bombing of North Vietnamese supply routes in Laos. But still he wavered when it came to Vietnam.

For a growing number of historians, Johnson's reluctance to escalate is explained by the interdependence of his Vietnam policy and his commitment to social reform at home. The war Johnson really wanted to fight was against poverty and inequality in the United States. He wanted to build what he called a Great Society, one in which voting rights and other basic civil liberties were extended to all Americans, regardless of colour; in which everyone would have access to education, housing and clean air; and in which health care was available as a right, not the privilege of those who could afford it. However, Johnson feared that a wholesale expansion of the US commitment to the other war, in Vietnam, would divert the nation's attention and resources away from the Great Society and, as a result, his legislative programme, moving through Congress in 1964–5, would stall. Worse, conservatives in Congress, inherently suspicious of Johnson's enthusiasm for reform, might even use the excuse of a widening war to kill off the Great Society altogether. Yet Johnson could not just abandon South Vietnam, either. 'I knew from the start that I was bound to be crucified either way I moved', he later explained:

> If I left the woman I really loved – the Great Society – in order to get involved with that bitch of a war on the other side of the world, then I would lose everything at home. All my programmes . . . But if I left that war and let the communists take over South Vietnam, then I would be seen as a coward and my nation would be seen as an appeaser, and we would both find it impossible to accomplish anything for anybody anywhere on the entire globe.
>
> (Young 1991, 106)

A choice could not be put off indefinitely, however. The moment of decision arrived on 7 February 1965 when a US air base at Pleiku was attacked by the Vietcong and nine Americans were killed, 130 wounded, and five aircraft destroyed. Johnson authorized immediate retaliatory raids against an area just north of the Demilitarized Zone (DMZ) – operation 'Flaming Dart' – but his advisers insisted it was not enough, and predictions about the survival of the RVN became gloomier than ever. The existing policy of waiting for stability in South Vietnam before taking direct action against North Vietnam was fast becoming a luxury that neither Saigon nor Washington could afford. The Vietcong were in the ascendant, street demonstrations against the undemocratic and repressive impositions of the military junta – and its dependency on America – were on the increase, and within the ruling Council itself the Generals continued to wage internecine political warfare. American observers began to fear the emergence from this chaos of a new neutralist government, responsive to the growing war-weariness and anti-Americanism of the population, that would bring the NLF into partnership and ask the United States to leave South Vietnam. But to the Johnson administration, as much as to the Kennedy administration before it, a neutral solution meant a communist solution, with the NLF (and by implication the communists) bound to dominate any coalition it entered and, in time, move towards reunification with North Vietnam.

In February 1965, therefore, the US government revised its earlier thinking and decided that only the bombing of North Vietnam – only a fulsome demonstration of America's commitment to South Vietnam – could help foster the desired stability and simultaneously ward off the spectre of neutralism. On 12 February, Johnson approved the sustained bombing of North Vietnam, operation 'Rolling Thunder'. On 27 February, the US State Department published a White Paper designed to justify the bombing. South Vietnam, it argued, was 'fighting for its life against a brutal campaign of terror and armed attack inspired, directed, supplied, and controlled by the communist regime in Hanoi' (Hess 1990, 85). On 2 March, 'Rolling Thunder' commenced. For Johnson, the doubts and reservations that had previously militated against escalation had now to be set alongside an inescapable reality: to do nothing would lead to a communist victory in South Vietnam, either militarily or, politically, via neutralization, and give rise to a domestic right-wing backlash just as, in 1949–50, the Truman administration had been castigated by Republicans for the 'loss' of China. One casualty of partisan political attacks seemed certain to be the President's cherished Great Society programme. It was with all of these considerations in mind that Johnson unleashed the United States Air Force against North Vietnam.

Thereafter, what Johnson feared came to pass. Far from buckling under the air bombardment, Hanoi remained resolute, refusing to negotiate on any basis other than a complete cessation of the bombing. Meanwhile, in the south, Vietcong military pressure intensified. In May, communist forces launched a large-scale offensive, meting out crippling defeats to ARVN units in several northern provinces. These reverses and accompanying mass desertions convinced American observers on the spot that the South Vietnamese army was close to complete collapse. Against this backdrop, the US Field Commander, General William Westmoreland, appealed to Washington for a ground troop commitment to stave off a disaster. In the two months following the inception of 'Rolling Thunder', around 75,000 American troops had arrived in South Vietnam, ostensibly to defend US air bases, but increasingly – and with Washington's tacit cognisance – engaging in offensive operations alongside the ARVN. Now, Westmoreland sought a further deployment of 100,000 men by October 1965, with perhaps another 100,000 early in 1966. He accompanied his request with a three-phase plan for turning the situation around. Phase I, secure US air and military bases, block the passage of North Vietnamese infiltrators into South Vietnam, and in this way halt the losing trend by the end of 1965; Phase II, move onto the offensive during 1966 by searching out and destroying the enemy's large main-force units in key rural areas, followed by pacification programmes to prevent liberated areas returning to communist control; and Phase III, confront the communists in their main base areas in a series of set-piece engagements, this phase to commence within eighteen months of the completion of Phase II.

Westmoreland's request led to instant Presidential authorization for aerial bombing of Vietcong-dominated areas of South Vietnam and, in Washington, to a month of intense deliberation, not about the assumptions underlying US involvement in Vietnam and whether further escalation should be undertaken, but about numbers. By midsummer 1965, the air war against the DRV had ensured that American credibility was inextricably linked in the eyes of the world to the survival of the Republic of Vietnam and, as such, Johnson's room for manoeuvre was virtually exhausted. The options of walking away ('bugging out') or neutralization were non-starters, but so was continuing the air war without serious bolstering actions in South Vietnam – to 'maintain present force and lose slowly', as Johnson put it. The alternative, to quote Johnson again, was to 'add 100,000 men – recognizing that may not be enough – and adding more next year'. At the end of July 1965, in deciding to meet Westmoreland's request, this was the course of action chosen by the President and his top advisers. Up to the last moment, however, it had been Johnson who kept asking the critical question: 'Are we starting something that in two to three years we simply can't finish?' (Kahin 1986, 379). But by this stage the equation had simplified: despatch troops and cling to the *possibility* of victory, or do nothing and accept the *certainty* of defeat and with it (according to the unquestioned logic of the domino theory) Chinese absorption of Vietnam and ultimately the whole of Southeast Asia. And whither the Great Society?

On 28 July 1965, Johnson duly informed the American people that he had decided to meet Westmoreland's immediate needs by sending 50,000 more troops to South Vietnam (bringing the total there to 125,000), and that if further forces were needed later they would be supplied as requested. By the end of the year, US military strength would total 184,314. And this was only the beginning.

CHAPTER FIVE

The American war, 1965–9

When historians refer to the Americanization of the Vietnam war, they normally take the summer of 1965 as its starting point – the moment when US forces assumed primary responsibility for combating the Vietcong and the ARVN was reduced to a predominantly supporting role. This, however, is military Americanization. Politically, the process began rather earlier, when Washington first used its influence in Saigon to promote a government that would resist the allure of neutralism and instead commit itself to unremitting war against the insurgents. For many politically-conscious South Vietnamese, neutralization had considerable attractions: the termination of an American presence that offended their patriotic sensibilities; an end to the insurgency and further bloodshed, even at the price of NLF participation in a coalition government; and the freedom to choose their own destiny, a luxury which the need to take sides in the Cold War did not allow. There was, moreover, widespread international support for a negotiated solution. But, as already seen, the US government regarded neutralization as a trap. According to the later testimony of Robert McNamara, it was assumed that South Vietnam 'would never be truly neutral, that it would be controlled by the North, and that this would, in effect, trigger the domino effect', leading to a communist-dominated Southeast Asia under Chinese auspices (McNamara 1995, 62). Mindful of these potentially grave consequences, Washington set itself against a neutral solution. American support for the coup against Diem in November 1963 had been partly inspired by this consideration. Then, when Diem's successor, General Duong Van Minh, also expressed a degree of sympathy for neutralization, he was promptly overthrown in another military coup at the end of January 1964.

American complicity in Minh's removal was widely suspected: McNamara was certainly satisfied with the outcome, predicting that the new South Vietnamese leader, General Nguyen Khanh, would be 'highly receptive to U.S. advice' (*Pentagon Papers*, III, 312). Over the next year, however, Khanh proved to be a serious disappointment in this regard. Assuming near dictatorial powers, he was loath to concede authority to civilian politicians, refused to introduce any meaningful reforms, used heavy-handed methods to put down popular demonstrations against the military junta, approved the mass arrest of political opponents, and spent more time defending his personal position against potential army rivals than fighting the communists. For the Johnson administration, these already troubling developments were compounded by indications that Khanh, like Minh before him, was desirous of a negotiated settlement with the NLF. His eventual removal from office in February 1965 was, therefore, a relief to US officials in Washington and Saigon, although it has been suggested that it was their increasingly open criticism of Khanh's rule that encouraged his opponents to move against him. A new government was formed with a civilian, Phan Huy Quat, at its head, but it was the ARVN that remained the political puppet master in Saigon.

One of the new government's first actions was to approve American plans for the bombing of North Vietnam. Because the United States had always insisted that it was acting in partnership with, not dictating to, the South Vietnamese, Saigon's sanction was an essential accompaniment to 'Rolling Thunder'. For the same reason, the Americanization of the war in the south could not proceed against the wishes of the RVN authorities, but on this matter Quat was less forthcoming. Possibly influenced by a new upsurge in neutralist sentiment, he temporized until, in June 1965, he was ousted by the military and power passed to Air Vice Marshal Nguyen Cao Ky and Army General Nguyen Van Thieu. Both men were ambitious, opportunistic and seemingly happy to allow the United States to take over the war effort in return for the benefits that possessing power brought with it. Thus, after more than eighteen months of shuffling the Saigon pack, the Americans had what they wanted, namely a native government that was anti-communist, anti-neutralist and willing to take orders. Late 1963, therefore, was the point at which the war began to be truly Americanized – the moment when, in defiance of the policy preferences of the Diem regime and its successors, as well as the wishes of many ordinary people in South Vietnam (and, surely, everyone in

North Vietnam), the United States determined to follow a course of action dictated by its own Cold War agenda.

In Hanoi, meanwhile, the opening months of 1965 found the Party leadership optimistic about the prospects for an early victory in the south. Politically, the Saigon government appeared weaker than ever, whilst popular support for a new neutralist coalition government (one that would inevitably be dominated by the NLF, hence the communists) continued to mount. Militarily, the Vietcong now possessed between thirty and forty-five main-force battalions, augmented by 10,000 North Vietnamese regulars, 35,000 southern guerrillas and up to 80,000 irregulars (Duiker 1996, 246). Controlling large swathes of the South Vietnamese countryside, the communist forces threatened to eradicate the ARVN as a going concern. In sum, all the indications were that the long-planned combined general offensive and uprising was near at hand and, with it, the final triumph of the Vietnamese revolution. But then came the US air offensive against North Vietnam and, shortly afterwards, the heavy influx of American combat forces, actions that were decisive in saving South Vietnam from total collapse. By the autumn of 1965, the Ky-Thieu regime, shielded by US military power, had managed to establish a measure of political stability, albeit through repressive and authoritarian action. For the communists, the prospect of the completion of their revolution, so tantalizingly close in the spring, had been replaced by the new reality of war with America.

In many ways, the strategies of Hanoi and Washington in 1965 were quite similar. North Vietnam's escalation was undertaken to hasten victory in the south but, failing that, to deter greater US involvement. It aimed to demonstrate to the Johnson administration that it had two choices: either a long and costly war should it decide to intervene in force to defend the southern Republic or, alternatively, a compromise settlement that allowed the United States to disengage and South Vietnam to develop politically in accordance with the NLF's programme. To strategists in Hanoi, the pattern of post-war US policy in Asia pointed towards acceptance of the latter option. Washington, after all, had balked at direct intervention on behalf of its beleaguered allies during the Chinese civil war, the Franco–Vietminh conflict and, more recently, the Laotian crisis. The Americans, Ho Chi Minh reflected, were 'practical and clear-sighted'. They would not 'pour their resources into Vietnam endlessly' (Hunt 1996, 85). Unusually for Ho, this proved to be a major error of judgement, one that seriously underestimated the importance that the US government attached to the preservation of an independent, non-communist South Vietnam. Interestingly, the aim of American escalation was based on almost identical assumptions – to prove to the enemy that it would pay a very high price for its interference in South Vietnam's affairs and so convince it to back off.

For the next three years, the United States fought what was officially termed a 'limited' war in Vietnam, involving the aerial bombardment of the north and extensive ground operations in the south. However, in retrospect, it is hard to see exactly what was limited about the American military effort. North Vietnam, for example, was bombed to such an extent that, by 1967, the US Joint Chiefs of Staff were to be heard complaining of 'target saturation' (Herring 1986, 176). In 1965, the US Air Force flew 55,000 sorties and dropped 33,000 tons of explosives on North Vietnam; in 1966, the sorties increased to 148,000 and the bomb tonnage to 128,000; and in 1967, 106,996 sorties, many flown by huge B-52 bombers, unleashed 247,140 tons of explosives (Lewy 1978, 381, 411). How, then, was the US government able to maintain that it was waging a 'limited' war?

Concern to avoid a wider war with Communist China ensured that American action was at least limited to *aerial* bombardment of North Vietnam and that a follow-up ground invasion was ruled out. During the spring and summer of 1965, the Johnson administration relayed secret assurances to Beijing underlining its desire to avoid a Sino–American confrontation. Beijing expressed a similar sentiment when replying that its armies would *only* enter the war if the United States invaded North Vietnam and thereby threatened China's security. This stand-off meant, in effect, that Hanoi's staunchest supporter implicitly encouraged its greatest adversary to bomb its territory (Qiang Zhai 1995/6, 233; Duiker 1995, 180). Whether the DRV government was aware of this compact is unclear, but it is worth noting that it was from this point onwards, as Sino–Soviet tensions intensified, that it began perceptibly to shift its allegiance towards Moscow. By the end of the decade, the Soviet Union would be North Vietnam's foremost benefactor. Given its abiding suspicion of Chinese intentions, as well as Beijing's record of placing self-interest before the furtherance of the Vietnamese revolution, this development may not have been entirely unwelcome to Hanoi.

The US air war against North Vietnam was also 'limited' in terms of targeting. President Johnson insisted that the heavily populated centres of the DRV's larger cities should be off-limits, and that care should be taken to keep civilian casualties to a minimum. These restrictions were obviously aimed at mollifying domestic and international opinion (the air war had aroused widespread condemnation from the very start), but Johnson was also keen to avoid killing or injuring Soviet or Chinese diplomatic/military personnel stationed in Hanoi and Haiphong and risking, as a result, a larger war by accident. Nor, at any stage, did the US Air Force aim to deliver a massive knock-out blow to all of North Vietnam's most important military-industrial targets. The objective, in the words of an American historian, was to push Hanoi towards and finally over the 'threshold of pain' (Lomperis 1984, 68). This was the point at which, in the interest of preserving something from what threatened to be the total wreck of its precious industrial base, North Vietnam would either sue for peace on American terms or disengage unilaterally from South Vietnam. Although the US Service Chiefs made known their unhappiness at this gradualist approach, they were obliged to accede to the dictates of the President and his civilian staff. Thus, in 1965, the bombing was restricted to military targets and infiltration routes in the southern half of North Vietnam; in 1966, the area of operations moved steadily northwards and took in new targets like petroleum storage depots and the transportation system; in 1967, steel factories and power plants and the outer environs of Hanoi and Haiphong were bombed; along the way, bombing pauses were introduced to give Hanoi the chance to reflect on the futility of continued resistance. Predictably, the Ho Chi Minh trail was subjected to tremendous bombardment, particularly in Laos, but this was never accompanied by follow-up ground operations. To the frustration of both the Joint Chiefs of Staff and General Westmoreland, President Johnson remained steadfast in his determination to keep the ground war confined to South Vietnam.

During the same period, the US government insisted it was fighting a 'limited' war in the south as well. Yet, between 1965 and 1968, more than a million tons of bombs were dropped on South Vietnam, at least twice the tonnage disgorged on North Vietnam. By the end of the 1960s, Vietnam as a whole had become the most bombed country in the history of warfare. If there was any sense in which the war in the south was 'limited', it was that the US troop commitment followed a drip-feed pattern. The Johnson White House allocated what it hoped would be sufficient force to achieve its objectives, and then added further increments when those objectives proved unattainable. By the end of 1965, there were just over 180,000 US military personnel in

South Vietnam; during 1966, the number doubled to approximately 360,000; by the end of 1967, the total stood at 485,000, and would peak in early 1968 at around 540,000. During the same period, the ARVN expanded to more than 800,000 men, but was relegated to a largely auxiliary status by a US Military Command contemptuous of its fighting prowess.

Apart from Washington's rejection of an invasion of North Vietnam, and its parrying of pressure from the military for permission to undertake 'hot pursuit' into neutral Laos and Cambodia, few operational restrictions were imposed on General Westmoreland. As already seen, the build up of American combat forces from mid-1965 helped stave off the near-certain collapse of the Saigon government and armed forces. Thereafter, the name of the game was attrition. With the bombing of North Vietnam and its supply lines supposedly helping to stifle the flow of arms and reinforcements into the south, US forces focused on wearing down the insurgents until a point was reached – what Westmoreland called the 'cross-over' point – where the communists were losing men faster than they could replace them. When that moment arrived, major offensive operations would be undertaken to destroy Vietcong and North Vietnamese base areas, whereupon victory would (in theory) be secured. In pursuit of this goal, a variety of attritional methods were employed; the use of massive air power, most notoriously the B-52 bomber, to pulverize communist-controlled areas and supply lines; the widespread employment of herbicides to destroy crops and deny food to the enemy; and the application of defoliants to strip the jungle canopy and forests and expose Vietcong concentrations. These, and other similarly destructive tactics, were utilized in support of the over-arching strategy of 'search-and-destroy', the main aim of which was to locate and then annihilate the enemy's large or main-force units.

Perhaps the main reason the US government felt justified in describing this enormous military effort as a 'limited' commitment was President Johnson's refusal to ask Congress for a formal declaration of war against North Vietnam. Instead, Johnson relied on his authority as Commander-in-Chief, augmented by the Gulf of Tonkin resolution, to wage war without technically ever being at war. This decision, one of the most controversial of his Presidency, has laid Johnson open to criticism from opponents and supporters of the Vietnam war alike. The former argue that he shied away from seeking Congressional approval because this would have led to a wide-ranging public debate about US policy with no certainty that the outcome would be approval for the kind of anti-communist war that he deemed necessary. Johnson, it is argued, escalated surreptitiously, despatching modest numbers of troops on a monthly basis deliberately to obscure the reality of the extensive commitment he was already wedded to. On the other hand, supporters of the US effort – those who believe that it was right and proper that America sought to save South Vietnam from communism – contend that Johnson should have welcomed a public debate, and insist that there was a consensus in favour of firm action if he had only sought it. His failure in this regard meant that when the war turned out to last far longer and cost much more than ever anticipated, an uninformed and perplexed American public reacted with understandable hostility to the continuation of the US commitment and its related sacrifices.[1]

Recently, a more sympathetic reading of Johnson's motives has emerged. At the heart of this interpretation is Johnson's personal conviction that a domestic consensus could indeed have been created in favour of a serious effort in Vietnam. Johnson, however, was worried that the deliberate cultivation of a national war mentality would generate intense public and Congressional pressure on him to go harder and faster in Vietnam than he believed to be wise or even necessary – if, as a result, he lost control of the pace and level of escalation, he feared that the risk of a wider war would be increased. The President was equally concerned that greater emphasis on Vietnam would destroy his dream of a Great Society in the United States. As Johnson appreciated, funding for an intensified war effort could only be found by denuding his domestic agenda, but any failure to allocate the necessary resources to Vietnam once America was formally at war would only encourage conservatives in Congress to kill off the Great Society altogether. Significantly, Johnson was never prepared to solve his dilemma by increased taxation out of fear that the American public would react with hostility to the cause – domestic social reform – that the heightened tax burden was designed to support. Johnson was therefore 'determined', he later recalled, to prevent Vietnam from 'shattering' the Great Society. To this end, 'I had no choice but to keep my foreign policy in the wings ... I knew that the day [Congress] exploded into a major debate on the war, that day would be the

---

[1]Between 1964 and 1968, a total of 222,351 US servicemen were either killed or wounded in Vietnam, see Lewy 1978, 146.

beginning of the end of the Great Society' (Kearns 1976, 283–4). This realization compelled Johnson to play down the scale and cost of the war in Vietnam. But however understandable his motivation, the result was an ever-widening credibility gap between what the administration said was happening and what the American public could see for itself on television news reports. For if, as Johnson maintained, Vietnam was not really a war at all, how was the destruction and the ever-rising number of young American dead to be explained?

Whether or not the American war in Vietnam was limited in theory – whether, as many disaffected Military figures later claimed, US forces in Vietnam were forced to fight with 'one hand tied behind their back' as a result of Washington's strictures – in practice, the degree of armed might that was brought to bear was quite staggering. Yet the war just dragged on and on, costly and inconclusive. The fact of American failure is now obvious, the reasons perhaps less so. Why did the withering bombardment meted out to it fail to coerce Hanoi into dropping its support for the NLF/Vietcong, or even lever it into negotiations on American terms? To begin with, the experience of the Second World War suggested that civilian morale was stiffened rather than broken by the ordeal of strategic bombing. In the case of North Vietnam, 'Rolling Thunder' appears to have drawn an already regimented and tight-knit society even closer together and helped rather than hindered Hanoi's efforts to mobilize the population in defence of themselves and their country. If American strategists had bothered to study Vietnamese history, such resilience in the face of an external threat might have been predicted. For more than a thousand years the Vietnamese had struggled to remain independent of a powerful China to the north, and a similar determination was evident in their more recent efforts to withstand the French and even the People's Republic of China. What was perhaps less expected was the limited impact the bombing would have on North Vietnam's capacity to supply men and weaponry for the war in the south. But, as the Americans discovered, the kind of bombing that would have brought a modern industrialized society quickly to its knees failed to disable a mostly agrarian country like North Vietnam. There were, for example, relatively few targets of great strategic importance, and those that there were, like fuel and oil installations, were widely dispersed to minimize damage.

Critically, much of the weaponry that bolstered DRV national defence or was filtered down the Ho Chi Minh trail to sustain the Vietcong, was not even produced in North Vietnam, but came from

China and the Soviet Union. President Johnson, given his concern about a wider war, was hardly going to authorize the US Air Force to attack the supply at source, nor even in transit. Soviet transport ships in the port of Haiphong might have been sunk before delivering their cargo, or the port itself, the principal point of entry for Soviet supplies, might have been mined, but Johnson consistently vetoed such suggestions. A major effort was made to destroy the Ho Chi Minh trail, but this, too, met with limited success as Hanoi assigned hundreds of thousands of repair workers to its upkeep. As for military manpower, thanks to conscription, North Vietnam could rely on 200,000 young men coming of military age each year, and it was able to despatch troops to the south in large numbers throughout the 1965–8 period. According to one respected survey, yearly infiltration rose from 12,400 in 1964, to 36,300 in 1965, to 92,287 in 1966, to 101,263 in 1967 (Lewy 1978, 66). The combined strength of the Vietcong and North Vietnamese in South Vietnam at the start of 1968 was put by US intelligence at around 300,000, but the total, including irregulars, may have been closer to 600,000. American and ARVN strength, meanwhile, stood at approximately 1.2 million (Lomperis 1984, 68). That Hanoi was able to make this kind of commitment to the south was due in no small part to the support of Communist China. As a result of the 1965 Sino–American stand-off, Beijing could be reasonably sure that North Vietnam would be spared a US ground invasion as long as its assistance continued to be indirect. Between 1965 and 1968, therefore, over 300,000 Chinese engineering and anti-aircraft technicians were employed in North Vietnam in the construction, maintenance and defence of the transport system and strategically important targets. This assistance freed up substantial North Vietnamese manpower for the war in the south and, crucially, for the repair of the Ho Chi Minh trail (Chen Jian 1995, 378–80).

Chinese material assistance was also lavish. Between 1965 and 1967, the North Vietnamese received *inter alia* over 500,000 guns and more than 4 million rounds of ammunition, 11,000 artillery pieces and 400,000 artillery shells (Chen Jian 1995, 379). But while China provided the bulk, the Soviet Union provided the quality – MiG fighters, anti-aircraft guns and surface-to-air missiles – that enabled North Vietnam to develop a highly effective air defence system which, by 1967, had accounted for over 900 US aircraft at a cost to the American treasury of $6 billion. By then, Soviet and Chinese assistance combined had topped $2 billion (Hess 1990, 94–5). There was, in addition, the moral cost to be paid for the bombing. Less quantifiable than the direct financial cost, it was none the less extremely high. By 1968, denunciation of American actions in the international sphere were increasingly echoed within the United States itself, as more and more people expressed an instinctive disgust at the spectacle of a military-industrial superpower blowing a backward peasant country to pieces.

As for the war in the south, by late 1967, although the American military effort had clearly knocked the communists off-balance, it had failed to deliver a really decisive blow and a bitter and bloody stalemate had developed. Why was the United States unable to prevail? The explanations offered by historians and military analysts are various and complex, but there is broad agreement that the Americans erred badly in focusing to an inordinate degree on finding a military solution to a problem that was as much political as it was military. Pacification – securing the allegiance of the civilian population, particularly in the countryside – was never the priority it should have been. Instead of trying to break the link between the rural population and the insurgents through imaginative political initiatives, American strategists evidently concluded that the comprehensive military defeat of the communists would solve everything. In fact, the failure to win South Vietnamese 'hearts and minds' would prove to be one of the main reasons why such a military victory never materialized.

There were, however, additional factors at work. As the French had earlier learned, superior firepower was of little value if the enemy refused to do battle on appropriate terms and suitable terrain, and the Americans soon grew frustrated as the Vietcong adopted the tactics that had served the Vietminh so well. Avoiding large-scale set-piece confrontations and concentrating instead on hit-and-run ambushes that steadily eroded US strength, albeit at considerable cost to themselves, the communists managed to maintain the battlefield initiative. Of the numerous and predominantly small-unit battles that took place between 1965 and 1968, nearly 90 per cent were initiated by the Vietcong or North Vietnamese (Hess 1990, 97–8). Even when worsted in battle, communist forces avoided complete destruction by simply melting away into the forests or mountains, or by retreating to their sanctuaries in 'neutral' Laos or Cambodia to recover and prepare for the next engagement. A further negative consequence of the American preoccupation with 'search-and-destroy' was that little attention was paid to consolidating control of those areas 'liberated' from the communists. Once US and South Vietnamese forces moved on, the communists would gradually return, and further costly operations would be required to clean up the area again. This failing was another symptom of the low priority accorded to pacification. Given that the aim of the North Vietnamese and Vietcong was to undermine both US military morale in Vietnam and public backing for the war in America via a strategy of protracted debilitating warfare, this approach played straight into their hands. So, in its way, did the increasingly indiscriminate use of US military power: the bombing of South Vietnam resulted in two civilian deaths for every insurgent killed, while 'search-and-destroy' sweeps cost the lives of six civilians for every identifiable communist killed, all of which assisted Vietcong recruitment (LaFeber 1993, 250). Crop denial, defoliation and 'free-fire zones' led to a huge exodus from the countryside, with perhaps as many as four million people (a quarter of the RVN's population) flooding into the cities to live in safer but cramped and miserable conditions.

American prospects were not improved by the behaviour of the Saigon government. Whilst proving more durable than its predecessors, the rule of Ky and Thieu was authoritarian, repressive and undemocratic. In 1966, discontent with the military junta spilled over into open Buddhist-orchestrated street protests in a number of cities. The government responded by sending in the army to restore order, which it did with speed and crude efficiency. In Washington, the Johnson administration played down the episode. Whereas Diem's repression of the Buddhists in 1963 did much to lose him the support of America, the Ky–Thieu regime's actions were condoned because the protesters, in addition to calling for democratic reforms, were also demanding an end to American intervention and a neutralist political solution. Johnson and his advisers, still convinced that neutralism was a euphemism for communism, argued in public that the protesters were Vietcong *agents provocateurs*, but in truth the disturbances were symptomatic of the abiding unpopularity of the Saigon regime. Neither Ky nor Thieu (who assumed power in his own right in 1967) could ever pose as a credible patriotic-nationalist alternative to the NLF/Vietcong whilst they were so obviously dependent on, and answerable to, a foreign power.

During the latter part of 1967, the US government, ignoring signs that the war had become a stalemate, insisted in public that significant progress was being made. There were some private doubts: McNamara, for example, wracked with guilt about the human cost of the bombing of North Vietnam, convinced that its continuation was

81

pointless, and concerned that the war in the south could drag on inconclusively for years, had resigned from the administration. But, by-and-large, Johnson, Westmoreland and others maintained a confident outward appearance, drawing encouragement from signs that the 'cross-over' point was close at hand. The 'body count' was the principal gauge of progress, but other indicators – enemy desertion and defection rates, for example, or weapons-loss ratio – were also used. And, by late 1967, all the statistics seemed to be saying the same thing: Westmoreland's attrition strategy was working and the war was being won. However, it is now clear that the data on which this conclusion was based was badly flawed. The 'body-count', for example, may have been exaggerated by up to thirty per cent by the inclusion of non-combatants amongst the enemy dead. Sometimes numbers were just invented, either by American units under pressure to meet kill quotas, or by ARVN officers keen to keep their US ally happy. According to rather more reliable estimates produced since the end of the war, around 180,000 Vietcong or North Vietnamese were killed in action in 1965–7, roughly three times the losses sustained by the Americans and South Vietnamese in the same period. Yet, as a result of infiltration from the north, and recruitment efforts in the south, overall communist strength was sustained during this same period, and may even have increased slightly. The 'body count' was, therefore, no guide at all to the proximity of the 'cross-over' point. But, at the time, it was the only one the Americans had.

There is, interestingly, a school of thought which suggests that Johnson and those around him were aware that statistical indicators were unreliable, but chose to mask inner anxieties with outward optimism in order to contain the growing anti-war movement in the United States. In other words, offering the American public the prospect of victory was intended to keep the lid on the pressure cooker of popular discontent about the war. Some limited opposition to American policy on moral grounds had pre-dated 1965, but protest really burgeoned once the bombing of North Vietnam began and, more especially, once US troops were committed to combat, the dissent growing thereafter in direct relation to the deepening of American involvement. The term anti-war movement is, however, a misnomer. So disparate were its elements, so diverse were the reasons for protesting against US escalation, that it is perhaps more appropriate to refer to a 'movement of movements' (Hess 1994, 255). Broadly-speaking, opponents of the war fell into three groups. The first comprised pacifists and others who objected to the war on grounds of conscience. Then there were what might be termed the radicals: often located on university campuses, they were deeply critical not just of the war, but of the political system that spawned it, a system that purported to be democratic yet denied basic civil rights to many American citizens because of the colour of their skin, and underpinned a dollar-driven foreign policy that encompassed support for anti-democratic right-wing regimes in the Third World. Lastly, there were the anti-war liberals, by far the largest component in the movement. Without wishing to challenge the system *per se*, this grouping argued that by backing an authoritarian government in South Vietnam, the United States, far from furthering democracy, was in fact betraying its own democratic principles.

Between 1965 and 1968, the anti-war movement became highly vocal and visible, its activities widely reported by the US and world media. Anti-war rallies increased in number and size as the Johnson administration plunged ever deeper into Vietnam, culminating in October 1967 when anywhere between 300,000 and half-a-million people rallied in New York, while in Washington demonstrators besieged the Pentagon. When it comes to assessing the importance of the anti-war movement, however, historians are divided. Whilst protest leaders later claimed that they helped prevent greater escalation and violence, it is difficult to ascertain just how far President Johnson allowed his policy choices to be dictated by what was happening on the streets of America's cities. Although Johnson clearly had a domestic audience in mind in his repeated public insistence that he would welcome a peaceful solution to the conflict, in private, neither Johnson nor his advisers expressed any real desire to negotiate until a position of political and military strength had been reached in Vietnam. Hence, whenever potential peace openings collapsed, the Johnson administration was quick to cover its domestic rear by blaming communist – and never its own – intransigence. This said, the North Vietnamese also indulged in public relations chicanery. Determined to maintain international sympathy by publicly emphasizing its desire for compromise, Hanoi, in practice, was just as committed as Washington to the principle of negotiating from strength, a position that was beyond the communists in the 1965–8 period. Consequently, military stalemate generated diplomatic stalemate, with both the Americans and North Vietnamese engaging in vituperative onus-shifting in their public explanations of the impasse.

Ironically, the anti-war movement's greatest impact was probably on North Vietnamese rather than American politico-military decision-making in that it encouraged Hanoi to believe that if they held out long enough, public disenchantment with the war would eventually force the US government to terminate its military commitment to South Vietnam. This, at any rate, was the signal that President Johnson felt the protesters were sending to Hanoi, and his ill-concealed contempt for the anti-war movement derived in large measure from his conviction that its activities implicitly – even explicitly – invited Vietnamese communists to continue killing American soldiers. However, opinion polls in 1967 would also have told Johnson that a substantial majority of the public, though deeply troubled, was still prepared to see the struggle through to its end. As such, the protesters were not representative of American opinion as a whole. To ensure that they never *became* representative, Johnson may have been compelled to make optimistic public statements that the end was in sight, even though the evidence of progress assembled for him by his advisers perhaps warranted greater circumspection.

So widespread was the belief that an important American and South Vietnamese breakthrough was imminent that, in December 1967, the US embassy in Saigon even inscribed invitations to its New Year's Eve party with the injunction, 'Come and see the light at the end of the tunnel' (Stoessinger 1979, 194). Exactly one month later, on 31 January 1968, the onset of the great communist Tet offensive gave the Americans the rudest of awakenings. Timing their action to coincide with the traditional lull in fighting that accompanied the lunar new year holiday of Tet, the Vietcong, supported by North Vietnamese forces, their combined numbers totalling around 80,000, took the war out of the countryside and into the major urban centres of South Vietnam, to the very heart of RVN and US strength. Thirty-six of the country's forty-four provincial capitals and sixty-four of its district towns were targeted in a series of massive co-ordinated attacks. In Saigon, communist guerrillas even penetrated the compound of the US embassy, their audacity witnessed by millions on television in America. Nor was this the extent of the offensive. In the countryside, thousands of villages and hamlets were seized. For an enemy supposedly on the verge of defeat, it was quite an achievement. Suddenly, nowhere in South Vietnam was safe from the insurgents. Although US military intelligence had been expecting an intensification of communist activity for some time, the assumption was that it would occur in the northern provinces of South Vietnam. In late 1967, large North Vietnamese units were reported within striking distance of a forward American base at Khesanh, just below the DMZ. Westmoreland, attracted by the chance to confront the enemy *en masse* and deliver a telling blow, committed large forces to the defence of the base. On 21 January 1968, the North Vietnamese duly laid siege, deploying 20,000 troops against the 6,000 marines inside the redoubt. However, though the battle would be drawn-out and, for the communists, extremely costly in life, it proved in the end to be merely a diversionary tactic that drew American forces away from the defence of the towns and cities further south and greatly facilitated communist infiltration efforts in the critical weeks leading up to Tet.

Strategists in Hanoi probably reacted to a combination of pressures and perceived opportunities in deciding to mount the Tet offensive. By the end of 1967, the stalemate in South Vietnam had begun to take its toll on communist resources, physical and material. North Vietnam's determination to match US escalation and superior firepower by sustained offensive action based on permanently high force levels had resulted in very heavy casualty levels, particularly for the Vietcong. Vietcong physical recovery was hampered by the depopulation of the countryside, as more and more people sought sanctuary in the cities, while Vietcong morale, already dented, may not have been particularly boosted by the arrival of ever larger numbers of northern 'fillers' and their domination of what the southerners had come to regard as their own revolutionary cause. From Hanoi's standpoint, therefore, the situation in the south, though not critical, was not good either. The obvious way to relieve the pressure on the Vietcong was to engineer the overthrow of the Thieu regime and its replacement by a new coalition dominated by the NLF and so under *de facto* communist direction. This new South Vietnamese government would then terminate the US presence and set in train negotiations with North Vietnam that would lead to eventual reunification. Next to this, the best hope was a unilateral US withdrawal brought on by an upsurge in anti-war protest in America. But if either scenario was to materialize, a military spectacular was the essential pre-requisite. However, from a more positive standpoint, some historians have argued that the weakness and unpopularity of the Thieu government in Saigon was now so pronounced that, in December 1967, the VWP Politburo concluded that the time had come to launch the projected general military offensive and political uprising. General Giap was given overall operational command. Hence, according to this interpretation, the Tet offensive was the product, not of communist unease about the future, but of optimism. Additionally, with Ho Chi Minh now frail and weak, the desire to present him with a united and communist Vietnam before he died may have played a part in the VWP's decision to launch the offensive.

Few historians dispute that Tet was a great turning point, but what *kind* of a turning point was it? In terms of profit-or-loss on the battle-field, it proved immensely costly to the communists who may have lost as many as 40,000 men, the great majority of them from the ranks of the Vietcong. US and ARVN forces regained control of most urban centres within a day or so, though it took a fortnight to restore full control of Saigon and a month of fierce fighting to secure Hué. As of 31 March 1968, US losses stood at around 1,000, the ARVN's at approximately 2,000. In addition, some 14,000 civilians had died, and more than one million new refugees had been created (Duiker 1996, 295; Herring 1986, 191). The offensive continued at a localized but still intense level until mid-summer, but well before then it was apparent that the communists had suffered not just an horrendous military dis-aster, but a severe political set-back insofar as they had failed to bring about a popular uprising against the Saigon government; failed, that was, to effect the *combined* general offensive and political rebellion they had been working towards for years. When, however, General Westmoreland, supported by the Joint Chiefs of Staff, asked President Johnson for 206,000 more troops to maintain the advantage in the field, his request was turned down. As Westmoreland later lamented, Tet 'could have been the turning point for success, but it was the turning point of failure' (Maclear 1981, 220).

What lay behind Johnson's decision to end escalation at this critical juncture? One factor was the state of American public opinion which, having listened for more than a year to official assurances that the war was being won, had now to come to terms with images from South Vietnam that suggested, at worst, that the US government had been lying about the reality of the situation, and at best, that Johnson and his advisers had not known what that reality was. Tet, however, left few Americans in any doubt about the *future* reality: continued sacri-fice without apparent end. The Johnson administration's public standing, even its competence to govern, were all called into question, with the attack from the media particularly damning. General West-moreland, among others, later claimed that biased reporting by liberal anti-war press and television journalists had turned public opinion against the war by depicting Tet as a defeat rather than a victory for US and ARVN forces, but such charges miss the point. If the war was being won, as Westmoreland said it was, Tet should never have happened. Thus it was the fact of the offensive rather than its outcome that was really important.

By late March 1968, the question confronting the Johnson administration was whether further escalation was possible in the light of public opposition and signs of rising Congressional disquiet with what was seen more and more as a Presidential war, one conducted without the approval of the American people and their political representatives. Johnson had been personally sympathetic to Westmoreland's request for reinforcements but deferred a final decision until he had sounded out his most trusted counsellors. To this end, Johnson established a Tet Task Force, led by his close friend and new Secretary of Defense Clark Clifford. On 25 March, Clifford and the so-called Wise Men presented their majority verdict: complete military victory was probably unattainable, certainly at an acceptable cost in blood and treasure. Even the continuation of a defensive war would be unpopular, not to say enormously damaging to the economy. Vietnam was already costing the United States close on $30 billion a year, had led to inflation at home and a weakening of the dollar abroad and had contributed to a budget deficit of $25 billion. For every dollar of bomb damage done to North Vietnam, the United States paid $9.60. The time had come for the United States to cut its losses and end the war. It was, Clifford told the President, 'a real loser' (Hess 1990, 95; Maclear 1981, 218).

Had Johnson retained the support of the Wise Men, he might have defied public opinion and persisted in Vietnam, even at the risk of damage to his Presidential re-election prospects in November 1968, but their desertion in combination with the public, political and media outcry forced him into a change of policy. The decision to reject further escalation was the beginning of the process. Then, on 31 March, Johnson publicly announced an immediate partial halt to the bombing of North Vietnam, with the prospect of a full cessation if Hanoi was prepared to engage in meaningful peace talks. Johnson's televised address to the nation also included the shock news that he would not be running for a second term as President. The pursuit of peace was more important, he said, than personal partisan causes. Thus, in one of the great paradoxes of the conflict, a shattering communist military defeat did more than any previous communist battlefield success to alter the course of American policy. Tet also ended the political career of perhaps the most committed liberal social-reformist US President of modern times. If, therefore, the offensive was indeed conceived in Hanoi with one eye on its potential impact on the American domestic political scene, it must be considered a most remarkable triumph.

CHAPTER SIX

A war of peace, 1969–75

The North Vietnamese, clearly keen for a complete end to the American air war, responded positively to President Johnson's call for peace talks, and preliminary exchanges began in Paris in May 1968. In South Vietnam, meanwhile, the war intensified rather than diminished as both sides sought military gains to use as diplomatic bargaining chips. The US Air Force, now denied a northern outlet, transferred its bomb payloads exclusively to southern targets in support of widespread ground operations. None of this heightened military activity led to progress in Paris, however, where the Americans demanded concessions from the DRV in return for a total bombing halt, and the North Vietnamese insisted that a full cessation of the air war was the prerequisite to dialogue on any other matter.

In the United States, meanwhile, the Republican Richard Nixon was elected President in November 1968. Inevitably, Vietnam played a big role in the run-up to the election, with Nixon claiming to be in possession of a 'secret' plan to end the war, though in truth this was merely vote-catching rhetoric. What Nixon undoubtedly *did* possess, however, was a determination to extricate US forces from Vietnam whilst simultaneously avoiding the reality or even the appearance of defeat, but it was only during his first months in office that he and his national security adviser, Henry Kissinger, actually evolved a 'plan' for achieving this objective. The starting point was to be the progressive withdrawal of all American ground troops (and eventually air and naval forces) in tandem with the transfer of defence responsibility to the South Vietnamese army. By giving tangible evidence of his desire to 'bring the boys home' from Vietnam, Nixon also hoped to draw the sting of the anti-war movement. Ground force disengagement would be paralleled by severe military pressure on North Vietnam designed to lever Hanoi into accepting a negotiated settlement on American terms, one of which would be a pledge renouncing all claims on South Vietnam. The final element in the equation was to be diplomatic efforts to persuade Moscow and Beijing to end their material assistance to the North Vietnamese which, if successful, would help speed up full American disengagement. However, as a consequence of the Tet offensive, Nixon was under pressure to achieve quick results. Neither the American public nor the US Congress was now in a mood to accept protracted war, and might even agree to a settlement on any terms if the conflict dragged on. But 'peace', for Nixon, meant 'peace with honor'. Anything less, he feared, would destroy America's credibility as a world power, dismay its allies and encourage its enemies. Lastly, because his political antennae told him that ending the war (or at least America's part in it) was the key to securing a second term as President in 1972, Nixon clearly had a more personal time-factor to consider as well.

In June 1969, Nixon met South Vietnam's President, Nguyen Van Thieu, at Midway Island in the Pacific and informed him that 25,000 US troops were to be recalled immediately, with more to follow by the end of the year. This was the start of the Vietnamization of the war, the removal of American forces *pari passu* with the expansion of the ARVN and its gradual assumption of the security burden. If judged solely in terms of US troop withdrawals, Vietnamization was a success. The year-end figures speak for themselves: 540,000 in 1968, 480,000 in 1969, 280,000 in 1970, 140,000 in 1971, and 24,000 in 1972. The inevitable corollary was a marked decline in US casualties, from 3,000 a week in 1968 to just one per day by late 1972, a development that helped neutralize the anti-war movement in America. A further and equally inevitable consequence was a rise in ARVN losses, which averaged 20,000 per annum between 1969 and 1971 and led Nixon's critics to charge that Vietnamization amounted to little more than 'changing the colour of the corpses' (Karnow 1983, 684–6; Hess 1990, 117). But the real test of Vietnamization was always going to be the ability of South Vietnam to defend itself unaided. Indeed, a complete American withdrawal could not take place until this was proven. Given that the expansion, training and equipping of the ARVN would not occur overnight, it was apparent that such proof would take time in coming. The dilemma for the Nixon administration, therefore, was how to implement swift and substantial cuts in American force levels if the South Vietnamese armed forces could not yet be relied on to hold the line against the communists. The answer arrived at was to deter any renewed North Vietnamese or Vietcong offensives through the application of firm military pressures. If the communists were placed on the defensive, time could be bought to perfect Vietnamization and continue US troop withdrawals.

The tried-and-tested (and so far failed) method of reducing the potency of the communist threat in South Vietnam was to bomb North Vietnam. But in 1969, a formal resumption of the air war was out of the question given the agitated state of American opinion. Instead, American strategists chose to concentrate on destroying communist supply-lines, munitions depots and sanctuaries in eastern Cambodia, a geographical extension of the war that President Johnson had resisted. Beginning in March 1969, Operation 'Menu' lasted for fourteen months and resulted in 3,600 B-52 sorties and the dropping of 100,000 tons of explosives on 'neutral' Cambodia (Hess 1990, 121). To avoid domestic and international denunciation, the US government went to great lengths to keep the bombing a secret and, extraordinary as it may seem, it largely succeeded. North Vietnam could not denounce the bombing without revealing the presence of its forces in Cambodia in defiance of the neutrality clauses of the 1954 Geneva agreements, clauses which, for propaganda purposes, it had always insisted it respected whilst criticizing Washington and Saigon for their violations. The neutralist Cambodian government of Prince Norodom Sihanouk was too weak to evict the Vietnamese and too compromised to denounce the US bombing: to protest openly would reveal what was being bombed and so embarrass Hanoi and invite either a North Vietnamese invasion or, more likely, North Vietnamese support for the Cambodian communists, the Khmer Rouge, in their campaign of violence against the Phnom Penh authorities.

However, the situation in Cambodia was dramatically altered in March 1970 when Sihanouk was ousted from power by his pro-American Prime Minister, General Lon Nol. North Vietnam reacted by extending open support to the Khmer Rouge, and then by consolidating its grip on the Cambodian–South Vietnamese border area. The latter move prompted Lon Nol to appeal to Saigon for assistance in destroying Vietnamese sanctuaries. In April, with Cambodian neutrality clearly at an end, the Americans and South Vietnamese acceded to this request and despatched a 30,000 man task-force. President Nixon, in a television address to the American people, justified the operation by arguing that the destruction of communist sanctuaries would hamper their preparations for an anticipated offensive against Saigon and thereby protect both US troop withdrawals and the Vietnamization programme. An additional objective, he said, was to find and destroy the Central Office for South Vietnam (COSVN), the communist 'Pentagon', believed to be located in the border fringes (Gettleman 1995, 452–5).

In spite of Nixon's broadcast, there was an immediate public outcry in the United States, with many people unable to understand how widening the war could bring about its end. Anti-war sentiment had not disappeared with the first US troop cuts, but it had been contained. Now, protest again gathered pace and intensity, particularly on university campuses where, in early May, four student protesters were shot dead by National Guardsmen at Kent State University in Ohio, and another two at Jackson State College, Mississippi. Even so, opinion polls suggested that there was still significant support for Nixon's handling of Vietnam from what he termed 'the great silent majority' of Americans, and as troop reductions continued apace during the rest of 1970, the protests gradually ebbed. On Capitol Hill, however, disenchantment with the war mounted, fuelled by a sense of collective guilt on the part of Congress at the supine surrender of so much of its constitutional power to the White House in 1964, and a related conviction that the ensuing disaster in Vietnam was primarily a Presidential war. The invasion of Cambodia presented Congress with an opportunity to reassert its lost authority that it was quick to seize, passing legislation that forced Nixon to withdraw the US invasion force by 1 July 1970 regardless of whether its objectives had been secured. More curbs on Executive power soon followed. The Gulf of Tonkin resolution, the symbol of Presidential primacy over Congress, was finally revoked, and the Cooper–Church Amendment to the Foreign Military Sales Act of 1969 (which had banned the use of American ground forces in Laos and Thailand) was extended to cover Cambodia, although in its failure to outlaw the use of US air power it inadvertently allowed the Nixon administration to continue its bombing campaign against that country.

Overall, the invasion of Cambodia achieved mixed results. Communist supply lines were seriously disrupted and a large amount of weaponry captured, and it is sometimes suggested that the absence of a major communist offensive in South Vietnam in 1970 or 1971 may have been due to US and ARVN spoiling tactics. There is, however, little firm evidence that such an offensive was being planned at a time when the Vietcong was recovering from its 1968 mauling. On the negative side, the invasion failed to locate the COSVN, led to a recrudescence of violent anti-war protest in the United States (which, even if subsequently quietened, must have added to Hanoi's determination to keep fighting), and produced sharp Congressional criticism of Nixon's Vietnam policy. It may even, in the opinion of some historians, have boosted the popularity of the Khmer Rouge and so aided its rise to power in Cambodia in 1975, with devastating consequences for the people of that country. As for Cambodia's neighbour, Laos, it too suffered as a result of events in Vietnam. Bombing of communist supply lines in Laos had begun under Johnson, with more than 450,000 tons of explosives dropped on the Ho Chi Minh trail and, increasingly, any area thought to be controlled by the communist Pathet Lao. Under Nixon, the bombing escalated: it is estimated that the tonnage dropped on Laos in the first two years of his Presidency surpassed the total for the whole of the Johnson period (Hess 1990, 124).

Despite the Cambodian misadventure, as 1971 dawned, the chances of Nixon making good his promise to end the war by the time he was due for re-election in 1972 seemed reasonable. Admittedly, doubts persisted about the ARVN's military prowess, but two years into Vietnamization it possessed numbers (almost a million men) and an arsenal sufficient, in theory at least, to counter a smaller and less well-equipped adversary. Moreover, with the communists on the defensive in the aftermath of the Tet offensive, the ARVN had been able to focus on pacification to a far greater degree than had been the case before 1969, and considerable progress had been made. At the end of January 1971, the American Military Command in Saigon approved an ARVN incursion into Laos (codename Lamson 719), partly to destroy troublesome communist sanctuaries, but also to test the maturity of both the Saigon armed forces and the Vietnamization programme. Congressional restrictions prohibited the use of American ground troops, but ARVN units (some 16,000 men) were given US air and artillery support. The operation began well, but ended in disaster, the ARVN encountering large North Vietnamese main-force units and sustaining heavy losses in a chaotic retreat at the end of March. So abject was the ARVN's performance that the Nixon administration was forced to conclude that Vietnamization was not working. Or, rather, that it was working in terms of troop withdrawals but not in terms of South Vietnam's ability to defend itself. Clearly, more time would be needed, but with no guarantee of Congressional and public support for a pro-longation of the war, and with the 1972 presidential election on the horizon, time was not on Nixon's side. In view of these considerations, the US government's subsequent increased level of interest in the stagnant Paris peace process now looks more like calculated pragma-tism than mere coincidence. In short, direct negotiations with North Vietnam were increasingly the only practicable method of a speedy end to American involvement in Vietnam.

Following the false start of May 1968, peace negotiations began in earnest in Paris in January 1969 between the United States, North Vietnam, Thieu's Republic of Vietnam and the Provisional Revolu-tionary Government (**PRG**) of South Vietnam, as the NLF leadership now styled itself in order to deal as equals with the other parties. However, the talks soon degenerated into a series of accusations and counter-accusations. Then, in August 1969, a series of secret meetings began, parallel to the public conference, between Henry Kissinger, the chief US negotiator, and senior North Vietnamese figures, principally (from February 1970) Le Duc Tho, a leading member of the Politburo. Yet for all the frankness of these secret discussions, it still proved impossible to reconcile the divergent US and North Vietnamese posi-tions. In summary, Hanoi's agenda included the following:

1) The withdrawal of all foreign troops from South Vietnam, meaning in practice the liquidation of the US military presence (Hanoi had never accepted the fiction of 'two' Vietnams and considered its forces in the south to be native rather than foreign, even though in public it consistently denied that they were there at all).

2) The construction thereafter of a new interim coalition govern-ment – in essence the PRG, which was dedicated to the fulfil-ment of the NLF programme – and free elections throughout South Vietnam.

3) Negotiations between the resulting Saigon administration and the North Vietnamese leading to reunification.

4) The exchange of all prisoners-of-war (**POWs**).

Implicit in Hanoi's demands was the prior removal of Thieu, regar-ded as the principal impediment to a negotiated settlement. As might be expected, the American position was rather different, and called for:

1) The departure of all non-South Vietnamese forces from the south (in other words a *mutual* US–North Vietnamese withdrawal).

2) North Vietnam to thereafter refrain from overt or covert interference in the affairs of South Vietnam.

3) Free elections in South Vietnam, which would remain an independent, separate state.

4) The return of all POWs.

These conditions bore the stamp of Thieu, who knew that the Americans were now desperate to rid themselves of their Vietnamese burden and so sought, as insurance, the firmest possible guarantees about South Vietnam's future. In doing so, Thieu played on the knowledge that Nixon could not conclude a settlement without his approval lest he – Nixon – be accused of betrayal or appeasement, charges he would want to avoid.

From 1969, therefore, Kissinger negotiated on the basis of what were Thieu's minimum terms. The North Vietnamese, for their part, showed no desire to meet those terms. In September 1969, Ho Chi Minh had died, but in his final Testament he encouraged those he left behind to remain loyal to their revolutionary ideals. 'Even though our people's struggle against US aggression, for national salvation, may have to go through more hardships and sacrifices', he wrote, 'we are bound to win total victory' (Ho Chi Minh 1973, 359–62). Given the immutability of Saigon's negotiating terms, therefore, and the inflexibility of Hanoi's position, diplomatic deadlock ensued. In an attempt to prise concessions from North Vietnam, the US government turned to the military option. Nixon sought to convince Hanoi that the alternative to compromise was the total destruction of North Vietnam through the practical realization of what he called the 'madman' theory. 'I want the North Vietnamese to believe I've reached the point where I might do *anything* to stop the war', he explained to an associate. 'We'll just slip the word to them that, "For God's sake, you know Nixon is obsessed about Communism. We can't restrain him when he's angry – and he has his hand on the nuclear button" – and [they will] be in Paris in two days begging for peace' (Haldeman 1978, 82–3). Powerful military action would also demonstrate that neither troop withdrawals nor anti-war protests in America had affected the US government's determination to safeguard a non-communist South Vietnam. Although not all historians accept that the 'madman' theory was a conscious stratagem, Hanoi could be forgiven for seeing an alarming irrationality at work in the decision to bomb and invade Cambodia, escalate the air war in Laos, and approve Lamson 719, certainly when compared to the more predictable targeting and bombing of the Johnson period. Yet, for all this, North Vietnam remained resolutely committed to its negotiating position during the first two years of the Nixon presidency.

This diplomatic stand-off was tolerable to the Nixon administration as long as Vietnamization remained a credible exit option. But then came Lamson 719 and, with it, grave doubts about Vietnamization and an altered perception of the value of the Paris peace process. This was clearly evidenced in May 1971 when Kissinger, in his back-channel contacts with Le Duc Tho, dropped his insistence on mutual withdrawal as a condition for any cease-fire and proposed instead a standstill cease-fire whereby South *and* North Vietnamese forces would remain in position but US forces would withdraw unilaterally. This was an extraordinary concession to make to an enemy in the context of negotiating the future security of an ally, but it was still not good enough for the North Vietnamese who continued to press for Thieu's removal from office. But there were, as seen, limits to how far Nixon could go in abandoning Thieu without being seen to abandon the cause that had cost America so dear. Therefore, with a negotiated settlement blocked by the obduracy of both America's ally and its enemy, and with Vietnamization experiencing serious difficulties, the prospects for 'peace with honor' had receded by the end of 1971.

There remained, however, the possibility that Nixon and Kissinger's wider foreign policy initiatives would yield a pay-off in Vietnam. Nixon had entered the White House convinced that the time was ripe for a fundamental re-evaluation of American Cold War policy, his political instincts reinforced by the intellectual judgements of the former academic Kissinger. What emerged was the concept of Détente – a concerted attempt to improve relations with the Soviet Union and thereby lessen the potential for superpower confrontation, limit the nuclear arms race, reduce the cripplingly high level of US defence expenditure and, not least, assist in ending the Vietnam war on a satisfactory basis. Nixon and Kissinger assumed that the Soviet Union would be interested in Détente for a number of reasons. First, having just reached a position of nuclear parity with the United States, Moscow could negotiate a strategic arms limitation treaty (**SALT**) from equality not inferiority. Secondly, this parity, though partly achieved by the slow-down in American missile programmes due to the inordinate demands of Vietnam, had been reached largely at the expense of investment in the domestic economy which had consequently stagnated. American policy-makers reasoned that Soviet difficulties could be ameliorated by an agreement that curbed the arms race and permitted the redirection of defence funds for domestic purposes, and by an expansion in US–Soviet trade, including the supply of much-needed modern technology, consumer goods and wheat. The United States would offer such trade, but on condition that Moscow concluded a SALT agreement and, in addition, helped resolve the American dilemma in Vietnam. Nixon and Kissinger were confident that the attractions of Détente were such that the Soviet leadership would be prepared to accept what became known as 'linkage'.

However, the US government possessed an additional inducement to ensure Soviet compliance, namely the China 'card'. By 1970 Soviet–Chinese antagonism – the Communist bloc's own Cold War – had reached boiling-point, with Moscow allegedly sounding out Washington on its likely reaction to a Soviet pre-emptive nuclear strike against China (Crockatt 1996, 207). This hostility was valuable to Nixon and Kissinger as they pursued Détente for, by cultivating improved relations with Beijing, they hoped to create the impression in Moscow of a nascent and threatening US–Chinese alignment. To forestall this development, the Soviet leadership would, it was believed, attempt to woo the United States which could then state its terms for co-operation (an arms control deal and assistance in solving the problem of Vietnam). China, for its part, was expected to engage in this 'triangular diplomacy' because, by the early 1970s, it seemed to fear the Soviet Union more than it did the United States and evidently saw co-operation with Washington as a potential safeguard in this respect.

The theory of Détente was not born fully-formed, but evolved gradually, only coming to fruition in February 1972 when Nixon made a much-publicized visit to China, met with Mao Zedong, agreed an expansion in bilateral trade, and set in train the process that would lead to full US–Chinese diplomatic relations in 1978. Significant as these achievements were, the real importance of the visit was the impression it made on the Soviet leader, Leonid Brezhnev. As Nixon and Kissinger intended, Brezhnev came under pressure to pursue a Soviet–American understanding to offset the dangers inherent in the Chinese–American alignment. Accordingly, at the end of May 1972,

Nixon, responding to an invitation from Brezhnev, became the first American President to visit the Soviet Union. The Moscow summit was notable for the conclusion of the SALT-1 agreement and a major expansion in American trade with the Soviet Union, including the supply of almost a quarter of the American wheat crop for 1972. The two powers also established certain 'basic principles' intended to govern their future relations and hopefully avoid direct or indirect confrontation.

This, then, was the high water mark of Détente. But what implications did it possess for Nixon's quest for 'peace with honor' in Vietnam? In June 1972, Chinese Premier Zhou Enlai told Kissinger that he was 'eager to remove the irritant of Vietnam from US–Chinese relations', and there is evidence that, in both 1971 and 1972, Beijing did bring pressure to bear on the North Vietnamese to offer concessions to the Americans in the Paris negotiations (Crockatt 1996, 248; Kissinger 1979, 1304). As the 1965 'stand-off' demonstrated, China had no desire to see the conflict in Vietnam escalate into a Sino–American conflict. Yet, in the end, Beijing never applied the ultimate sanction and terminated its assistance to the North Vietnamese. The Soviets, too, occasionally counselled restraint, but their material assistance to Hanoi actually increased during the Détente years. In maintaining their assistance to North Vietnam, it seems that neither Moscow nor Beijing was prepared to risk alienating a potential long-term ally in the Sino–Soviet struggle in pursuit of the greater but quite possibly short-lived backing of America. Of course the main beneficiaries of these tensions were the North Vietnamese who, by careful balancing diplomacy, managed to maintain aid from both sources. By the early 1970s, however, its traditional distrust of all things Chinese – communist or otherwise – combined with the fact that only the Soviet Union could provide the modern military equipment it needed, saw Hanoi tilt ever more decidedly towards the Moscow camp, and Sino–Vietnamese relations became strained. Thus, whatever hopes Nixon and Kissinger harboured that Détente would assist them in achieving 'peace with honor' were destined to come to nothing. By the spring of 1972, a direct deal with Hanoi remained the only feasible means of extrication before the November Presidential election.

In Vietnam, however, the communists appeared more intent on outright victory than in diplomatic solutions. Despite the set-back of Tet, the North Vietnamese leadership had never rejected the validity of its twin-track strategy of a general military offensive and popular political rising, rather, it was a matter of waiting until the strength of the revolutionary forces was sufficiently replenished to resume the charge. Interestingly, a number of recent analyses of the war have argued that, as a result of the experience of the Tet offensive, North Vietnamese strategists no longer regarded military and political action as *equally* important. Tet, by calling into question the premises underlying the 'People's War' philosophy, encouraged Hanoi to view armed force as the primary instrument of revolution – to accept, in other words, the Maoist dictum that political power grows out of the barrel of a gun, and to resort to regular, or conventional warfare.

At the start of 1972, with communist military strength sufficiently restored, Party strategists in Hanoi determined to mount a new offensive in the south. A number of considerations contributed to the decision to strike: with American support for Thieu holding firm, North Vietnam could expect little from the peace process unless the southern revolutionary forces could effect a shift in the military balance; in South Vietnam, US ground forces had almost completed their withdrawal leaving the ARVN more vulnerable than in 1968; and, politically, the Thieu regime remained as unpopular as ever. Even if a new offensive failed to achieve a decisive politico-military breakthrough, the experience of Tet pointed to a probable upsurge in anti-war feeling in the United States perhaps sufficient, in an election year, to produce the total and unilateral withdrawal of all remaining American ground, air and naval forces. Finally, there must have been some concern that as Détente progressed, Beijing and Moscow might yet be encouraged to desert North Vietnam, an understandable suspicion in the light of events at Geneva in 1954 when both communist powers elicited no compunction in sacrificing Vietnamese revolutionary interests for the sake of their own particularist foreign policy objectives.

At the end of March 1972, therefore, a force of 120,000 North Vietnamese troops, supported by Soviet-built tanks and artillery and backed by thousands of Vietcong guerrillas, launched what became known as the spring – or Easter – offensive across the DMZ. Taking US and South Vietnamese forces by surprise, the offensive initially made great progress. But American air power was soon employed to check the advance, and, on 16 April, Nixon ordered the formal resumption of the air war against North Vietnam. Over the next month, operation 'Linebacker' encompassed 700 B-52 sorties of tremendous intensity, including a 48-hour bombardment of the Hanoi–Haiphong complex, targets President Johnson had ignored from fear of the consequences if Soviet or Chinese personnel were killed or injured. Then, on 8 May, Nixon ordered the mining of Haiphong harbour, another escalatory option forsaken by Johnson as wantonly incendiary. When, as a result, a Soviet ship was sunk, Moscow refused to let the incident jeopardize the imminent Brezhnev–Nixon summit. Beijing, likewise wary of damaging improved relations with Washington, offered only muted condemnation of the bombing. Ironically, therefore, the strategy of Détente, predicated on peace, allowed the Nixon administration to wage war in Vietnam on a scale and with an abandon that Johnson, the great bomber of legend, could scarcely have credited. In the end, US air power was decisive in arresting the communist offensive some way short of Saigon and its overall politico-military objectives. When it was finally called off in June, communist losses were reckoned in the region of 100,000, more than double the figure that accompanied Tet (Summers 1984, 135).

Now came a time for reflection. In Hanoi, Party leaders were confirmed in their view that, for all its size, the ARVN was a poor adversary, and that only the continued presence of US air power had prevented the communists from taking advantage of their military superiority. A decision was taken, therefore, to make possible the total withdrawal of US forces from South Vietnam through a policy of concessions at the Paris negotiations. This did not, however, betoken Hanoi's abandonment of its revolutionary aims. On the contrary, it was regarded as a necessary tactical retreat to prepare for a future advance. Given the state of American public and political opinion, the chances of the Nixon administration securing popular support for a reactivation of its military involvement in Vietnam was clearly remote – and would become remoter still the greater the interval between US disengagement and the Hanoi's final push for victory in the south. As for the American government, it had been serious about a diplomatic settlement for some time, certainly since the failure of Lamson 719. Thus the Paris peace process, suspended when the spring offensive had opened, now resumed with the North Vietnamese willing to offer concessions and the Americans primed to receive them.

On 8 October 1972, in the back-channel discussions in Paris, Le Duc Tho at last conceded the retention of Thieu as South Vietnamese head of state as a condition of any cease-fire. In response, Kissinger restated his agreement to a standstill cease-fire, with North and South Vietnamese forces remaining in position, a complete American pullout within sixty days of an armistice, and a full exchange of POWs. In the days that followed, the political arrangements were sketched out. After US withdrawal, the Saigon regime and the PRG would recognize each other as legal entities, and then join with a third group of 'neutrals' in a National Council of Reconciliation and Concord (**NCRC**) to plan democratic elections in the south and, if the resultant government was so mandated, to move towards reunification with the north. During the transitional period, all areas under clear PRG–Vietcong control were to be acknowledged by the Saigon government, and vice versa. Hanoi agreed to end troop infiltration into the south, and accepted a continuation of limited American military aid to the RVN regime in the post-settlement period. Washington, for its part, would provide post-war reconstruction assistance for the whole of Vietnam.

On 21 October 1972, the world learned that a draft treaty had been worked out in Paris acceptable to Hanoi and Washington. The next day, operation 'Linebacker' was halted. On 23 October, Thieu denounced the provisional settlement, but this did not stop Kissinger announcing in public on 31 October that 'peace is at hand', nor Nixon's re-election on 7 November with a landslide majority. In retrospect, Nixon's victory had been assured for some time – probably since his visits to Beijing and Moscow had allowed him to bask in the glory of Cold War peace-maker – and the prospect of peace in Vietnam may have been a less decisive factor than he at one time imagined. Nevertheless, the domestic pressure on the US government to finalize the peace, having got so far, was now considerable, but to do so meant overcoming Thieu's objections. For, as Nixon understood, a separate peace remained taboo. Thieu himself was perfectly aware of the American dilemma. Peace would come, he said, 'when I sign the agreement' (Isaacs 1983, 46). Nixon attempted to bring that moment closer through Project Enhance Plus, a massive US airlift of military equipment, including hundreds of aircraft that made the South Vietnamese airforce the fourth largest in the world (Hess 1990, 132). He also offered generous post-war aid for reconstruction and, in a private letter on 14 November 1972, his 'absolute assurance that if Hanoi fails to abide by the terms of this agreement it is my intention to take swift and severe retaliatory action'. But Thieu would not budge and in fact supplied Washington with a list of sixty-nine specific objections to the proposed settlement.

Unable to move its ally, the United States next tried to shift its enemy. The North Vietnamese, however, were equally stubborn, arguing that an agreement had already been reached and that if the problem was Thieu, then it was an American problem. The dialogue was suspended in mid-December, whereupon Nixon ordered the resumption of the bombing of North Vietnam. Hanoi, anticipating another 'madman' act, had already commenced the evacuation of civilians from urban centres. On 18 December, operation 'Linebacker II' was launched, its timing leading it to be dubbed the Christmas bombing. Ironically – and tragically for the 2,196 Vietnamese who died and the 1,877 who were injured, as well as the 125 American servicemen either killed or listed as missing in action – the most intensive aerial bombardment of the entire war took place *after* the US and the DRV had reached an agreement on peace terms (Anderson 1993, 174). In eleven days of terror bombing, with only a brief pause on Christmas Day, the US Air Force dropped 40,000 tons of bombs, mostly on Hanoi and Haiphong. Nixon's public justification was that the North Vietnamese had sought to alter the settlement in their favour and, having failed to do so, had broken off the talks. The bombing was thus intended to bring them back to Paris. Nixon did not mention that the real cause of the breakdown was Saigon's intransigence. Indeed, perversely, the magnitude of the Christmas bombing can be seen as a venting of American frustration at the behaviour of an ally rather than an enemy. It was also clearly calculated to persuade the South Vietnamese government to accept the peace settlement by demonstrating the kind of retaliation the United States would employ if the communists broke its terms, and, by the same token, to dissuade North Vietnam from attempting any violations in the first place.

On 29 December, Hanoi signalled that it was ready to recommence negotiations if the United States halted the bombing. This Nixon agreed to, and Kissinger and Le Duc Tho returned to Paris. There, on 23 January 1973, they reached a provisional agreement, and then, on 27 January, a formal peace treaty was signed by representatives of the United States, the Democratic Republic of Vietnam, the Republic of Vietnam and the Provisional Revolutionary Government. The obvious conclusion to be drawn from this *dénouement* is that the Christmas bombing produced improved terms for the United States and South Vietnam. However, while Nixon claimed that it did make a difference and led to a 'peace with honor', the majority historical verdict is that the treaty, which included a standstill cease-fire and a unilateral American withdrawal from South Vietnam, was essentially that agreed between Kissinger and Le Duc Tho the previous autumn. If this is so, the real difference was Thieu's readiness to support in January

1973 what he had refused to support in October 1972. What, then, brought about his change of heart? Relentless American pressure, including promises of even greater post-war reconstruction aid laced with hints that a separate peace was no longer as objectionable as it once was, undoubtedly made some impression. But most commentators agree that the decisive factor was another – secret – assurance by Nixon that, in his own words, 'we will respond with full force should the settlement be violated by North Vietnam' (McMahon 1995, 564–5). On this basis was Thieu's assent secured and America's longest war ended. On 29 March, two months after the Paris accords were signed, the last American soldier left Vietnam.

Did the United States obtain 'peace with honor'? In attempting an answer to this question a number of points need to be borne in mind. First, the Paris accords only ended *American* involvement in the war, not the war itself. Indeed, the settlement broke down almost immediately, with neither the Saigon regime nor the PRG–Vietcong prepared to talk to each other about territorial delineation or election plans, and with their forces in close and tense proximity, military exchanges ensued. During the remainder of 1973, Thieu, working on the premise that territory equalled power, ordered the ARVN to seize 'contested' and even supposedly inviolate communist-dominated parts of the country, and by the start of 1974 he was claiming jurisdiction over 75 per cent of South Vietnam. But territorial control did not mean acceptance of his regime by the population at large. Nor, with the ARVN stretched to breaking point, was this level of control likely to last. The southern revolutionary forces, meanwhile, taking their lead from Hanoi, had reacted to Saigon's encroachments with only limited and defensive revolutionary violence, preserving their military strength for a new general offensive at an opportune point in the future. With this goal in mind, North Vietnam, disregarding the Paris treaty, continued to infiltrate men and supplies into the south. Meanwhile, in Laos and Cambodia – both ignored by the Paris settlement – fighting continued to rage between the American-backed anti-communist government forces and the native communist movements.

Thus Nixon's assertion about peace may be challenged. As for the issue of honour, this seems to hinge on the way in which Thieu was treated in the final phase of the peace negotiations and, by extension, on the existence or otherwise of a 'decent interval' mind-set in the Nixon White House. Critics of Nixon have argued that he made an empty promise to Thieu to secure his approval of the settlement, and that Nixon had no intention of re-opening American participation in the war when, as he expected, the peace eventually unravelled. If, however, there was a 'decent interval' between American withdrawal and a final North Vietnamese thrust, and if the United States continued in the intervening period to furnish the southern state with as much military hardware as it could accept, Nixon hoped that the subsequent and inevitable communist victory would be seen by the world to be a South Vietnamese rather than an American defeat. Those historians who take this view are however divided on whether 'decent interval' thinking was present in the Nixon White House from the very outset, or whether it evolved as a reaction to the growing realization in 1971–2 that Vietnamization was never really going to guarantee South Vietnam's future security. Either way, the United States was given an 'interval' of just two years – hopelessly insufficient to hide the reality of its own defeat alongside that of the South Vietnamese when, in April 1975, Saigon fell to the communists. Against this, Nixon's defenders maintain that the key promise to Thieu was given in all sincerity, but that subsequent events conspired to ensure that it could not be honoured. The first of these was, obviously enough, Nixon's resignation in August 1974 as a result of the Watergate scandal. The second was the Watergate-inspired Congressional backlash against all-things-Nixon and, more generally, against reopening involvement in a Presidential war. Nixon always insisted that it was the US Congress that undermined his plans for ensuring the survival of a non-communist South Vietnam, an assertion which, by implication, denies the existence of a 'decent interval' philosophy. South Vietnam's fate was sealed, Nixon attested, by a 'spasm of Congressional irresponsibility' (Crockatt 1996, 244). However, to judge the validity of this argument, it is necessary to examine events in both Vietnam and the United States in 1974–5.

As clashes between the Saigon government forces and the PRG–Vietcong escalated during 1974, Hanoi, as committed as ever to a united and communist Vietnam, resisted the temptation to return to full-scale revolutionary war. For one thing, more time was needed to reconstruct its armed forces following the losses incurred in 1972. For another, there remained the possibility that the Thieu regime might collapse in the face of internal political and economic pressures, thus obviating the need for renewed warfare. North Vietnam's caution was also dictated by the need to obtain assurances from the Soviet Union and China that their material support would continue in the future. By

late 1974, however, Hanoi evidently concluded that the time had come
to act. Thieu remained in power in Saigon. Soviet military assistance,
far from dropping off, had increased over the previous twelve months,
enabling the speedy reconstitution of North Vietnam's armed
strength. Above all, there was a growing conviction that the United
States would not re-open its part in the war. The Americans 'would
not come back', predicted DRV Premier Pham Van Dong, 'even if you
offered them candy' (Duiker 1995, 244).

How could the North Vietnamese be so certain of American quies-
cence? The answer, according to Nixon and his supporters, is that in
1973-4 Congress used its 'power of the purse' to block funding for
further US military action in the Indochinese theatre, thereby under-
mining the credibility of the deterrent strategy constructed by Nixon
and signalling to Hanoi that it could challenge the Paris peace accords
with impunity. Nixon has a circumstantial case. In 1973, Congress
indeed passed legislation that denied funds for *any* American combat
action in the Indochina region. Moreover, at the end of 1973, the War
Powers Act, approved over Nixon's veto, required that 'in every possible instance' the President should consult Congress before sending
US forces into battle. On those occasions when the Commander-in-
Chief believed immediate action was necessary, Congress was to be
given a full justification within two days, and if this was not sufficiently persuasive, the President would be given sixty days to withdraw US forces. An obvious practical test of this legislation would be a
surprise North Vietnamese attack on South Vietnam (Gettleman 1995,
490-5). Meanwhile, military assistance to South Vietnam was slashed
from $2.27 billion in fiscal year 1973 to $1 billion in fiscal 1974 to just
$700 million in fiscal 1975. According to one estimate, the ARVN
required close to $3 billion in material support per annum to function,
and by 1974-5 it was suffering from shortages of fuel, ammunition and
spare parts for its military vehicles (Duiker 1995, 242; Hess 1990, 138).

There seems little doubt that these actions helped convince the DRV
leadership that the United States would not respond to a renewed
offensive against South Vietnam, that it brought forward the timetable
for that offensive, and had a highly damaging effect on South Vietnamese morale in general and ARVN morale in particular. Yet Congress
would probably have acted similarly even if Nixon had remained in
office, for, as the branch of government closest to the people, its legislation merely reflected the overwhelming desire of most Americans
to confine the whole Vietnam experience to history. Nixon, the

consummate politician, would have been well aware of the direction in which opinion was moving when he gave his undertaking to Thieu about reopening the war – well aware, his critics would say, that he could make an empty promise to secure his short-term objective and, in the long-term, blame Congress for preventing him making it good.

In January 1975, North Vietnam launched what would develop into the Ho Chi Minh campaign, its last great offensive. From the outset, the campaign succeeded beyond Hanoi's most optimistic expectations as the ARVN began retreating before the advancing North Vietnamese main-force units and never stopped. Thieu appealed to the United States for help, but none was forthcoming. Nixon's successor, Gerald Ford, and Kissinger, now Secretary of State, tried to persuade Congress to commit substantial emergency military assistance to South Vietnam, but to no avail. Were their efforts animated by a belief that such assistance could yet halt the offensive? Or with a communist victory now certain, was the Ford administration continuing to indulge in the 'decent interval' subterfuge? Was it trying to demonstrate to American and world opinion that it had done, and was still doing, all it could to avert disaster, but if disaster came, it would be of South Vietnamese not American making? Either way, Congress refused the request. When General Alexander Haig, commander of NATO forces in Europe, pleaded with Ford to resume the air war against the north, the President replied: 'Al, I can't. The country is fed up with the war' (Duiker 1995, 246). On 21 April, Thieu, declaring to the world that America had betrayed him, fled the country. On 30 April 1975, Saigon fell to the advancing communist forces. Vietnam was reunited, independent and communist.

CHAPTER SEVEN

Conclusion

Today, more than two decades after the final communist triumph, historians continue to analyze the causes, chart the course and reflect on the consequences of this most violent of conflicts. Of the principal participants, an estimated half-a-million Vietnamese died during the French war of 1945–54, and anywhere between two and three million indigenous combatants and non-combatants during the later American war; French and French Union losses amounted to 75,000; and by 1975, United States war-dead had added a further 59,000 to the grim reckoning. However, the massive and still expanding body of historical literature devoted to Vietnam has led, not to a consensus on the origins and outcome of the conflict, but to a proliferation of rival interpretations and to what one historian has called an 'unending' debate (Hess 1994, 239–64). Until quite recently, this debate exhibited an unfortunate lack of balance, with the Vietnamese role in war banished to the periphery of the discussion, and an inordinate emphasis placed on examining American involvement, particularly in the 1965–73 period. Happily, over the past decade or so, matters have begun to improve in this regard. Writing in 1996, the American scholar, William J. Duiker, observed that:

... monographic studies, memoirs and documentary collections published in Vietnam and elsewhere are beginning to fill the gaps in our knowledge of the Vietnamese side of the conflict. These materials provide the researcher with a clearer picture of what decisions were made, who made them, and why. Although a number of crucial questions have not yet been resolved, we are today much closer to obtaining a balanced picture of the war as viewed from all sides, not just from Washington and Saigon but also from Hanoi, Moscow and Beijing.

(Duiker 1996, 3)

Recent research based on newly available Chinese communist sources, and on documents housed in the hitherto closed archives of the former Soviet Union, have also contributed to a more rounded evaluation of the conflict. However, it remains to be seen whether increased access to evidence on communist decision-making will help or hinder the search for consensus or merely generate new questions and more scope for disputation. Probably the latter. As the historiography of American Cold War policy demonstrates, the greater the quantity of primary source material, the greater the likelihood of competing and conflicting analyses. Indeed, the tremendous amount of legitimate evidence available to the historian of post-war international affairs makes it possible to construct a case in support of almost any reasonable contention. Hence there can never be 'right' (that is to say, definitive) answers, only 'right' questions.

With regard to the present study, the key questions are 1) what was the conflict actually about? and 2) why did it end the way it did? If it is agreed that Vietnam witnessed not one but several overlapping wars during the twentieth century – that Vietnam *wars* is a more appropriate description of what took place than the oft-used Vietnam *war* – a number of possible answers present themselves. At one level, the conflict began in 1945 as an attempt by a European colonial power to recover its former position in Southeast Asia, and erupted into a full-scale war of reconquest in December 1946. From the outset, however, the global Cold War complicated a primarily colonial issue. The need to cultivate good relations with France in Europe as an adjunct of the containment of potential Soviet expansionism helps explain the change in American policy in mid-1945, from opposition to any resumption of colonial rule in Vietnam to active assistance in the return of the French. Another reason why a colonial problem quickly assumed a Cold War dimension was that the Vietminh were led by Ho Chi Minh, a communist and former Comintern agent, with Communist Party members occupying other positions of influence in the movement. Ho and his comrades initially disguised their ideological preferences to prevent non-communist nationalist defections from the Vietminh that would diminish its patriotic legitimacy. Seeing through this smoke-screen, the French were quick to impress upon the Americans the vital role they were playing in Vietnam in helping contain the spread of Kremlin-directed international communism – and quick, too, to insist on American assistance in the task. Yet, in spite of its belief in the existence of a monolithic communist bloc, the strongly anti-colonial Truman administration was deterred from offering meaningful help in the late 1940s by the refusal of successive French governments to promise full independence for Vietnam.

During 1949, however, anti-communism began to overtake anti-colonialism as the driving force of American policy. Then, early in 1950, a combination of communist bloc recognition of the Vietminh, scathing attacks on its anti-communist credentials by domestic critics in the wake of the fall of China, and the reworking of the Containment strategy to incorporate embryonic 'domino' theory thinking, helped convince the Truman administration of the need for a more pro-active stance on Vietnam. In February, the French puppet government under Bao Dai was given diplomatic recognition, and in May a US military assistance programme was commenced which, by 1954, would be underwriting almost the entire financial cost of the French war effort. The outbreak of the Korean war in June 1950 appeared to confirm the rectitude of these decisions, and Vietnam thereafter became a vital element in the US Containment barrier in Asia. However, American military aid to France was effectively nullified by the start of Communist Chinese assistance for the Vietminh, and by the end of 1950, while the French and the Vietminh continued to confront one another as of old, the conflict had evolved into a Sino–American war-by-proxy and a potential catalyst for general war. Without ever losing its colonial character, Vietnam had become a Cold War problem of the first order.

As might be expected, the Vietnamese viewed the conflict rather differently. To begin with, the war that broke out in 1946 was merely the most recent manifestation of a centuries-old Vietnamese determination to resist external domination. For over one thousand years, the main threat had come from a large and powerful China to the north, but was superseded in the nineteenth century by French imperialism. By the 1870s, superior French firepower had helped subjugate Vietnam, Laos and Cambodia, the three countries coming together to form French Indochina. For the next fifty years, the French dealt harshly and effectively with all eruptions of anti-colonial protest. However, the fall of France in 1940, and more especially the spectacular Japanese conquests in Asia in 1941–2 at the expense of the colonial powers (the French in Indochina, the British in Malaya,

Singapore, Hong Kong and Burma, the Dutch in Indonesia), were destined to have profound consequences. Though itself defeated in 1945, Japan, by proving that the notion of white superiority was a myth, encouraged a generation of Asian nationalists to believe that European hegemony could be challenged. This was certainly true in Vietnam where, in 1946, the Vietminh mobilized to counter a colonial war of reconquest with a war of national liberation.

The desire for independence, and the ability and capacity to achieve it, were of course two different things. The Vietminh, in finally overcoming the French in 1954, clearly exhibited the latter attributes in abundance, but it was Ho Chi Minh and the communists who were primarily responsible for giving them substance. Before 1945, anti-colonial protest in Vietnam had been mainly rural, localized and aimed at the redress of basic socio-economic grievances rather than the overthrow of the ruling élite. What the communists brought to the Vietminh was strict discipline, organizational genius, a sophisticated approach to propaganda and recruitment, and above all a clear politico-military strategy for winning power. By the early 1950s, the Vietminh had developed into a highly efficient and co-ordinated nation-wide organization with a broad membership and widespread popular support under the inspiring leadership of Ho Chi Minh. Unlike their nationalist allies, however, the Vietnamese communists were fighting for more than an end to French rule; their ultimate aim was the construction of a socialist and eventually communist society. The French war was thus regarded by the communists as a true revolutionary war designed to realize the twin goals outlined in the Party's founding programme of 1930, namely independence and the restructuring of post-colonial Vietnam along Marxist–Leninist lines. As already seen, for the first (national) revolution to succeed – the prerequisite for the success of the second (social) revolution – the communists deemed it necessary to keep their ideological aspirations under close wraps.

Following the climactic events of 1954, the conflict underwent another transformation. The colonial war was ended. Or, rather, the *French* colonial war, for there are historians, most of them operating on the left of the political spectrum, who view American policy in South Vietnam after 1954 as neo-colonial in intent. One problem with this analysis, however, is that Ngo Dinh Diem, the power in Saigon until 1963, was hardly a 'front man' for US imperialism. Indeed, so resistant was he to American advice, and so dictatorial was his rule, that the United States might well have abandoned South Vietnam had overriding Cold War imperatives not dictated otherwise. Having seen the northern half of Vietnam 'lost' in 1954, both the Eisenhower and Kennedy administrations determined to make a stand in the south. Committed to the Containment doctrine, in thrall to the Doomsday logic of the domino theory, and convinced that the Vietnamese communists were acting on an agenda drawn up in Beijing and/or Moscow, neither administration seriously questioned the need for an extensive US commitment. As historian George C. Herring has observed, American involvement in Vietnam was 'the logical, if not inevitable, outgrowth of a world view and a policy, the policy of Containment, which Americans in and out of government accepted without serious question for more than two decades' (Herring 1986, xii).

The Cold War complexion of the problem was reinforced in the 1950s by on-going military and economic assistance to North Vietnam from China and the Soviet Union. With the onset of the communist-led insurgency against the Diem regime in 1959–60, however, the struggle in South Vietnam began to display the characteristics of a civil war, with southerner pitted against southerner. Even as North Vietnamese support for the insurgents mounted during the early 1960s, the war retained an essentially southern imprint: although Hanoi supplied arms and other material assistance to the Vietcong, recruitment was drawn from native southern stock, whilst the troops infiltrated into the south before 1965 were almost exclusively southern-born 'returnees' who had regrouped in the north at the time of partition. North Vietnam went to such lengths to obscure its role in the insurgency in part to appease its Chinese and Soviet backers, both of whom feared being sucked into a wider war if more openly aggressive tactics resulted in serious American reprisals. But keeping the US role limited was, for Hanoi, an obvious and sensible end in itself. Washington looked on North and South Vietnam as two separate countries, even though the Final Declaration of the 1954 Geneva Conference explicitly stated that the partition line was provisional and should not be interpreted as constituting a political or territorial boundary. Hanoi naturally endorsed the Geneva view of Vietnam as one country temporarily divided, but for pragmatic reasons it chose not to challenge the American interpretation by *openly* aiding and directing the insurgents. To do so would allow Washington to claim 'external' aggression and justify a greater commitment to the defence of South Vietnam. Instead,

North Vietnam operated at a covert level in support of the NLF and Vietcong. The goal of the southern revolutionary forces was a combined general offensive and popular uprising that would sweep the US-backed regime from power. Then a new coalition government, dominated by the popular NLF (thus, by extension, the communists) would move to resurrect the Geneva settlement, organize all-Vietnam elections, and arrange for national reunification.

In mid-1964, however, with the South Vietnamese government and armed forces apparently in terminal decline, Party leaders in Hanoi succumbed to vaulting ambition and despatched regiments of the regular North Vietnamese army to the battle-front. The prospect of securing a swift and complete victory in the south was seemingly irresistible. Yet, in retrospect, Hanoi gambled and lost. Defying all expectations, the Saigon regime held back the revolutionary tide long enough for US air power to be employed against North Vietnam, and for US combat troops to arrive to stabilise the position in the south. In the process, the war reinvented itself. From the American standpoint, by the end of 1965, a low-level effort to counter a guerrilla-based insurgency had widened into a large-scale effort to save South Vietnam from total disintegration in the face of what was seen as direct North Vietnamese aggression. It was, simultaneously, a war to prevent Communist Chinese expansion into Southeast Asia, for Washington persisted in regarding the Vietnamese communists as proxies of Beijing rather than independent-minded revolutionaries working to their own nationalist agenda. 'Over this war and all of Asia', declared President Johnson in April 1965, 'is another reality: the deepening shadow of Communist China' (McMahon 1995, 210).

Such was the tenacity with which official Washington adhered to the dogma of Containment and the domino theory that the decision to escalate in 1965 – to shore up the acknowledged trigger-domino of Southeast Asia – was taken because it was believed to be in America's national security interest to do so. But was it also in the interest of the people Washington claimed to be helping, the South Vietnamese? This is still an under-researched area, but there is none the less sufficient evidence to sustain the troubling possibility that the American war was just that, a war wanted by the American government but *unwanted* by a substantial majority of politically-conscious South Vietnamese. Among the urban and educated strata of society, neutralization was the increasingly favoured solution in the 1963–5 period, but Washington never offered the South Vietnamese a choice between war and peace. Convinced that any neutralist coalition would be subverted by the communists, the Americans spent the eighteen months following Diem's death in an increasingly desperate search for a government in Saigon that shared its outlook. Nothing, President Johnson averred, was more important than 'knocking down the idea of neutralization wherever it rears its ugly head' (*FRUS 1964*, I, 185). In the summer of 1965, Washington at last found what it was looking for in the shape of the 'Young Turks', Ky and Thieu. But in this matter, as in so many others, the Ky–Thieu regime was hardly representative of the hopes and aspirations of the population at large.

If the character of the war had changed for the Americans and South Vietnamese, it obviously changed for the communists, too. To use Hanoi's terminology, 1965 witnessed the transition from 'special war' (in which the United States relied on the South Vietnamese to do the fighting) to 'limited war' (wherein American forces took a direct and leading role in the south, and expanded the theatre of operations to the north). The North Vietnamese refuted the charge that their own escalation in 1964–5 amounted to aggression, external or otherwise. On the contrary, if Hanoi's 'one nation divided' viewpoint is accepted, it was the United States that was guilty of aggression and of undue – outside – interference in an intra-Vietnam conflict. The American war was, on this reading, a continuation of the struggle for national liberation begun in 1946 but only half-completed in 1954, as well as an attempt to extend the socialist transformation of Vietnam, accomplished in the north between 1954 and 1960, to the whole of the country.

By 1965, Vietnam had also become an informal front in a different kind of Cold War, the one being waged between Communist China and the Soviet Union for the leadership of World Communism. Moscow and Beijing both fêted Hanoi in an attempt to secure an ally in their increasingly bitter dispute. Between 1950 and 1965, the Chinese had been the main supporter of the Vietnamese revolution. The Soviet Union, whilst sympathetic to Hanoi's position, remained somewhat aloof, particularly in the post-Stalin period when 'peaceful co-existence' with the West was the *leitmotif* of Soviet foreign policy. However, following the overthrow of Nikita Khrushchev in October 1964, Soviet policy became far more activist as the new Kremlin leadership attempted to reclaim from the Chinese the mantle of revolutionary militancy in the Third World. Beijing, in turn, sought to match increased Soviet aid to North Vietnam with greater assistance of its own. Whilst it was clearly in Hanoi's interest to avoid committing itself either way in the Sino–Soviet conflict, by the late 1960s its relations with the Soviet Union were undoubtedly better than those with China. This was partly because only Moscow could supply the sophisticated weaponry it had come to rely on for its air defence, but it also reflected the age-old suspicion that China sought dominion over Vietnam, a fear that fraternal socialist ties from 1949–50 onwards had failed to diminish.

Just as the term Vietnam *war* does not do justice to the multi-faceted nature of the conflict up to and including 1965, it retained its variegated character in the years that followed. For combatants and non-combatants alike in the south, it became a deadly war of attrition. To the North Vietnamese, the start of the US 'Rolling Thunder' campaign meant that the war of national liberation that was already underway was merged with a war of national survival. For President Lyndon Johnson, the situation in Indochina became a distraction from the war he really wanted to fight against poverty, social injustice and racial inequality in the United States. In fact, by 1967, Vietnam had become more than a distraction – it had proven the destroyer of the Great Society. As the black civil rights leader, the Reverend Martin Luther King, Jr, emphasized in a speech in April 1967, the war in Vietnam was increasingly waged at the expense of the underprivileged in the United States. Johnson's domestic legislative programme of 1963–5 had held out 'a real promise of hope for the poor – both black and white', King remembered:

> Then came the build-up in Vietnam, and I watched the program broken and eviscerated as if it were some idle political plaything of a society gone mad on war, and I knew that America would never invest the necessary funds or energies in rehabilitation of its poor so long as Vietnam continued to draw men and skills and money like some demonic, destructive suction tube. So I was increasingly compelled to see the war as an enemy of the poor and to attack it as such.

> (Gettleman 1995, 311)

In the United States, Vietnam became the first 'television' war, with uncensored depictions of the fighting and destruction beamed into millions of homes on a daily basis. These images – the spectacle of the world's most powerful nation destroying a small peasant society –

contributed to the crisis of conscience that many ordinary Americans felt about the conflict. Again, Martin Luther King spoke for many people when he insisted that it was incumbent upon the United States to find a peaceful solution. 'If we do not act', he concluded, 'we shall surely be dragged down the long, dark and shameful corridors of time reserved for those who possess power without compassion, might without morality, and strength without sight' (Gettleman 1995, 318).

Troubled though many Americans were by the war, anti-war protest, whilst vocal and high-profile, was held in check by official assurances that progress was being made and that an end was in sight. Then came the Tet offensive of 1968, the shattering of public confidence in the administration and, within the President's policy-making circle, the rapid conversion of hawks into doves. Before the desertion of Clark Clifford and the so-called Wise Men, the President had planned to begin his 31 March address to the nation with the words, 'I want to talk to you about the *war* in South Vietnam'. In the event, his speech opened with 'Good evening, my fellow Americans: Tonight I want to speak to you of *peace* in Vietnam ...'. The alteration in wording went far beyond semantics: the American war had been put into reverse. Henceforth, it was a question of how the United States escaped from, rather than ploughed ever deeper into, Vietnam. Even so, 1968 was also the year that the fighting in Indochina was mirrored to a hitherto unprecedented degree on the streets of American cities, culminating in the riots surrounding the Democratic National Convention in Chicago in August.

The Tet offensive also altered the North Vietnamese and Vietcong perception of the war. In particular, its outcome cast doubt over the validity of the 'People's War' strategy adhered to by the Vietnamese communists since the 1940s. The Vietminh and its successors had always maintained that their efforts were on behalf of the Vietnamese people. When the moment came to embark on the final stage of the revolutionary process, the combined general offensive and uprising, 'people power' was expected to play a critical role in delivering victory. The Tet offensive was a test of 'People's War', but it was a test that failed. The rural and urban population did not rise up *en masse* in support of the revolutionary forces, and so left them militarily exposed. According to a communist post-mortem, the revolutionary zeal of the people proved far weaker than anticipated and the offensive on its own was unable 'to arouse the enthusiasm required to put unrelenting pressure on the enemy' (Duiker 1995, 214). Weaker, however, did not mean non-existent, as the more optimistic American assessments contended. For the non-combatant in South Vietnam, the war had become a matter of survival. Villagers living in contested areas, for example, would have been foolish in the extreme to declare their support for the revolution until it became clear that the Vietcong was going to prevail. To reveal overt sympathy for the insurgents and then find one's village passing back into Saigon government control was to lay oneself open to violent reprisals. This is an over-simplification, undoubtedly, but consistent none the less with non-combatant behaviour in other civil wars where territory passed from one side to another with some regularity.

For the communists, then, Tet proved to be both a political set-back and a military calamity. Yet, in triggering the chain of events in the United States that led to the end of US escalation and the start of the Paris peace process, the offensive proved, in the long-term, to be a great victory for Hanoi and its southern supporters. It would be wrong, though, to suggest that from 1968 the communists simply jettisoned their established politico-military strategic principles. True, the next major offensive, the North Vietnamese thrust across the DMZ in the spring of 1972, was a wholly conventional military assault. So, too, was the final great offensive of 1975 that overwhelmed Saigon and swept the communists to power. But political groundwork remained vitally important. Hanoi perhaps no longer relied on 'people power' to supplement its military strategy to the degree it did before Tet, but without sustained political efforts in urban and rural South Vietnam between 1968 and 1975 aimed at rebuilding the revolutionary infrastructure and retaining popular support, the final communist victory might not have come as speedily and completely as it did.

For the Americans, extricating themselves from Vietnam proved far harder than getting involved in the first place. To borrow historian Alistair Horne's description of the French war in Algeria, from 1968 onwards the United States waged a 'savage war of peace' (Horne 1978). Given the Nixon administration's determination to achieve 'peace with honor', and given that this could best be secured through success on the battlefield, there was in practice little to distinguish the scale of the American war effort either side of the Tet watershed, save in the suspension of the bombing of North Vietnam (until May 1972), and in the Vietnamization of the ground war in the south. In some ways the conflict actually escalated parallel to American efforts to de-escalate their involvement. Geographically, it was widened to take in the rest of Indochina, whilst the bombing of North Vietnam in 1972 reached previously unscaled heights of severity. All in all, according to one critic, the Nixon approach was a disaster:

> Some of the direct results were: a prolongation of the war by four years, at immense cost in lives and treasure; double-digit inflation, previously unknown in the United States; more bitterness, division, and dissension among the American people; the flouting of the Constitution by a President as he secretly extended the war to Laos and Cambodia, with tragic results for the people of both countries; and the eventual loss of the war.
>
> (Ambrose 1993, 240)

The reality of the American defeat in 1975 alongside that of the South Vietnamese is inescapable. But as William Duiker has lately observed, perhaps 'the most significant fact about the conflict is not that the United States lost but that the Communists won' (Duiker 1995, 251). Historians, in seeking to explain this outcome, have advanced a wide variety of theories, ranging from the superior organizational ability of the communists and their use of terror to intimidate opponents, through to the importance of the nationalist legitimacy the Communist Party acquired during the war against France and the inspirational leadership of Ho Chi Minh. However, though these factors all played their part, Duiker believes that the key to the communist victory is to be found in the 'genius' of the Party's programme and strategy. The political programme of the Vietminh, for example, was carefully designed to advance communist ideological objectives by linking them to 'the most dynamic forces in Vietnamese society', namely the desire for economic and social justice and the drive for national independence. By this means, the Vietminh – and by extension the communists – secured the support of a broad spectrum of the Vietnamese population in the struggle to overturn French rule, a breadth of constituency that a straight appeal to Marxism-Leninism could never have matched. In helping to make the national revolution, however, this popular constituency also presented the Party with the freedom to effect its own social revolution, at least in North Vietnam. Later, in the 1960s, the National Liberation Front for South Vietnam – likewise under hidden communist direction – adopted a similar programme for similar reasons and was similarly successful in mobilizing a mass popular base to confront the United States and its agents in Saigon.

117

Duiker also believes that the Communist Party's 'People's War' strategy was touched by 'genius'. Noteworthy for its extreme flexibility, it 'relied on a combination of political and military techniques in both urban and rural areas with a diplomatic and psychological offensive that undermined public support for the party's rivals, in France and the United States as well as in Vietnam itself'. When, in the mid-1960s, the conflict escalated into a direct military confrontation with the United States, Hanoi's 'strategic objective was not to win a total victory on the battlefield, but to bring about a psychological triumph over its adversaries, leading to a negotiated settlement under terms favourable to the revolution'. In this, the Vietnamese communists were undoubtedly successful (Duiker 1995, 251–8). Their triumph, however, owed much to Ho Chi Minh, without whom 'there might not have been a Vietnamese revolution'. Ho was an 'unusual composite of moral leader and organizational genius, half Gandhi, half Lenin', Duiker concludes. It was 'a dynamic combination' (Duiker 1996, 359–60).

Whilst it is right and proper to accentuate the positive contribution made by the Vietnamese communists to the victory of their own revolution, it is none the less difficult to deny that the French, and more especially the Americans, were to a large extent the architects of their own defeat. The French, for example, in waging a colonial war as part of a general effort to recover their national power and prestige following the traumatic experience of World War II, were clearly swimming against the tide of history. 'Colonialism is dying out', Ho Chi Minh had declared in 1945. 'Nothing will be able to withstand world pressure for independence' (*Pentagon Papers* 1971, I, 51). By 1954, the French in Vietnam had tried to prove Ho wrong and had failed, and were about to try again – and fail again – in Algeria. But what of the United States? Given the collective Cold War mentality of policy-makers in Washington, there was a certain inevitability about the way in which the United States took over from the French as the principal enemy of Vietnamese independence. From the Eisenhower administration's standpoint, Ho Chi Minh was a communist, and the Vietminh a communist organization receiving and responding to orders from Moscow by way of Beijing. At a time when crude images of a monolithic communist bloc dominated American strategic thinking, the idea that Vietnam might develop into an *independent* communist state was given little consideration. It followed that a Vietminh victory at the 1956 all-Vietnam elections would constitute a significant advance for international communism at the expense of the 'free' world. Moreover, the logic of the domino theory suggested that the advance would not stop there, for a communist Vietnam seemed certain to contaminate its neighbours, leading to the communization of Southeast Asia as a whole. To forestall this development, the United States set out under Eisenhower to contain Vietnamese communism, the perceived vehicle of Sino–Soviet expansionism.

As earlier suggested, the US Cold War strategy of Containment offers a convincing explanation for American intervention in Vietnam, but it provides few insights into why, once fully engaged in the 1960s, the United States was unable to prevail. In this connection, historians have devised a number of interpretative frameworks. One of these is the Quagmire thesis, according to which successive American Presidents approved decisions relating to Vietnam in splendid ignorance of their consequences. Gradually, cumulatively and inexorably, these decisions led to entrapment in an unwinnable war. However, a counter-argument is provided by stalemate theorists, who contend that the critical decisions regarding US intervention were taken by the White House – particularly in the Kennedy–Johnson period – in the full knowledge that none of them would achieve victory because victory was not the goal. Instead, US Presidents, for dubious and self-serving political reasons, sought only to avoid defeat. As summarized by Robert Divine, this thesis rests on 'the traumatic impact' of the loss of China in 1949 on the United States in general and on the Democratic Party in particular. Neither Kennedy nor Johnson, as Democrat Presidents, wanted to risk a repeat of that experience, hence 'anything was preferable to defeat in Vietnam, even a deliberate stalemate' (Divine 1988, 81–3).

In recent years, a growing number of historians, whilst accepting that the net result of US policy choices in Vietnam was indeed a stalemate that led eventually to defeat, have sought to rehabilitate the reputation of Lyndon Johnson. The main focus of attention has been the motivation behind his decision to do, in his own words, 'what will be enough, but not too much' to achieve American objectives (Herring 1986, 142). One obvious reason was his concern to avoid a wider war involving Communist China and possibly even the Soviet Union. Another was his deeply held desire to see his Great Society programme come to fruition, an ambition that necessitated the careful shepherding of finite budgetary resources and, more importantly, the maintenance of liberal *and* conservative support in Congress. To do too little or too much in defence of South Vietnam would destroy the political consensus on which the successful passage of his domestic legislation depended, hence Johnson's preference for a middle-of-the-road policy in Vietnam, one that eschewed the extremes of all-out war and disengagement. Yet, as Larry Berman has written, this proved to be a disastrous compromise, for Johnson 'committed the United States to fight a limited war against an enemy totally committed to revolutionary war'. On the other hand, this revised assessment of Presidential motivation does at least offer 'a far more appealing portrait of LBJ as a leader caught in a genuine dilemma rather than as a political manipulator deceiving the American people' (Divine 1988, 90–1).

More recently still, Robert McNamara, in a cathartic and highly controversial memoir on the war, has written that he and other US policy-makers in the 1960s 'underestimated the power of nationalism to motivate a people (in this case, the North Vietnamese and the Vietcong) to fight and die for their beliefs and values'. This, though, was just one mistake amongst many:

> We both overestimated the effect of South Vietnam's loss on the security of the West and failed to adhere to the fundamental principle that, in the final analysis, if the South Vietnamese were to be saved, they had to win the war themselves. Straying from this central truth, we built a progressively more massive effort on an inherently unstable foundation. External military force cannot substitute for the political order and stability that must be forged *by* a people *for* themselves.
>
> (McNamara 1995, 323, 333)

When it was published in 1995, McNamara's account aroused both admiration and criticism in the United States – admiration for its honesty and frankness, criticism because it fell short of offering an apology for what took place and provided instead a list of excuses or explanations for American failure. As Marilyn Young has pointed out, although McNamara acknowledges that the war was 'wrong, terribly wrong', he goes on to argue that the errors that he and his fellow policy-makers made were 'not of values and intentions but of judgment and capabilities'. To Young, this suggests that 'the wrongness was about practice, not principle' (McNamara 1995, xvi; Young 1996, 440). It would appear, therefore, that more than twenty years after the fall of Saigon, McNamara – and perhaps many Americans – have yet to decide whether the war was wrong because it was wrong, or wrong because America lost.

The Vietnam war was many wars, overlapping, interlocking and often interdependent. With the communist triumph in April 1975, however, one last variant was added to the list, for the fall of Saigon proved that the conflict had been a revolutionary war in the most literal sense – a circular process ending at its point of departure. In September 1945, Ho Chi Minh had declared:

> Viet-Nam has the right to be a free and independent country – and in fact it is so already. The entire Vietnamese people are determined to mobilize all their physical and mental strength, to sacrifice their lives and property in order to safeguard their independence and liberty.
>
> (Fall 1967, 141–3)

First France and then the United States sought to contest this claim, albeit for differing reasons. Both failed because both ignored the warning that Ho attached to his declaration. The Vietnamese people were indeed ready to 'sacrifice their lives and property in order to safeguard their independence and liberty'. The tragedy was that it took nearly thirty years of such sacrifice for them to get back to where they had been in September 1945. But, then again, it was a tragedy for all concerned.

Glossary

ARVN	Army of the Republic of Vietnam
CIA	Central Intelligence Agency
COSVN	Central Office for South Vietnam
DMZ	Demilitarized Zone
DRV	Democratic Republic of Vietnam
ICP	Indochinese Communist Party
MAAG	Military Assistance Advisory Group
MACV	Military Assistance Command, Vietnam
NATO	North Atlantic Treaty Organization
NCRC	National Council of Reconciliation and Concord
NLF	National Liberation Front
NSAM	National Security Action Memorandum
NSC	National Security Council
OSS	Office of Strategic Services
PAVN	People's Army of Vietnam
PLAF	People's Liberation Armed Forces
POW	Prisoner/s of War
PRC	People's Republic of China
PRG	Provisional Revolutionary Government
PRP	People's Revolutionary Party
RVN	Republic of Vietnam
SALT	Strategic Arms Limitation Talks/Treaty
SEATO	Southeast Asia Treaty Organization
VWP	Vietnam Workers' Party

Select bibliography

Ambrose, S. *Rise to Globalism: American Foreign Policy since 1938* (London: Penguin, 1993).

Anderson, D. *Shadow on the White House: Presidents and the Vietnam War, 1945–75* (Kansas: University of Kansas Press, 1993).

Bergerud, E. *The Dynamics of Defeat: The Vietnam War in Hau Nghia Province* (Boulder, Colorado: Westview, 1991).

Berman, L. *Planning a Tragedy: The Americanization of the War in Vietnam* (New York: Norton, 1982).

Berman, L. *Lyndon Johnson's War* (New York: Norton, 1989).

Bui Tin *Following Ho Chi Minh: The Memoirs of a North Vietnamese Colonel* (Honolulu: University of Hawaii Press, 1995).

Buttinger, J. *A Dragon Defiant: A Short History of Vietnam* (Newton Abbot: David & Charles, 1973).

Cable, L. *Unholy Grail: The US and the Wars in Vietnam, 1965–68* (London: Routledge, 1991).

Cameron, A. (ed.) *Vietnam Crisis: A Documentary History* (2 volumes, Ithica: Cornell University Press, 1971).

Capps, W. (ed.) *The Vietnam Reader* (London: Routledge, 1990).

Chen Jian 'China's Involvement in the Vietnam War, 1964–69', *The China Quarterly*, Vol. 142, 1995.

Chomsky, N. *Rethinking Camelot: JFK, the Vietnam War, and US Political Culture* (London: Verso, 1993).

Clayton, A. *The Wars of French Decolonization* (London: Longman, 1994).

Commager, H. (ed.) *Documents of American History: Volume II, Since 1898* (New York: Appletone–Century-Crofts, 1968).

Crockatt, R. *The Fifty Years War: the United States and Soviet Union in World Politics, 1941–1991* (London: Routledge, 1996).

Dalloz, J. *The War in Indochina, 1945–1954* (New York: Barnes & Noble, 1990).

Divine, R. 'Vietnam reconsidered', *Diplomatic History*, 12/1, 1988.

Duiker, W. *Vietnam: Nation in Revolution* (Boulder, Colorado: Westview, 1983).

Duiker, W. *Sacred War: Nationalism and Revolution in a Divided Vietnam* (New York: McGraw-Hill, 1995).

Duiker, W. *The Communist Road to Power in Vietnam* (Boulder, Colorado: Westview, 2nd edn, 1996).

Errington, E. & McKercher, B. (eds) *The Vietnam War as History* (New York: Praeger, 1990).

Fall, B. (ed.) *Ho Chi Minh on Revolution: Selected Writings, 1920–66* (New York: Praeger, 1967).

Fenn, C. *Ho Chi Minh* (London: Studa Vista, 1973).

Folliot, D. (ed.) *Documents on International Affairs, 1954* (Oxford: Oxford University Press, 1957).

Gaddis, J. *Strategies of Containment: A Critical Appraisal of Postwar American National Security Policy* (Oxford: Oxford University Press, 1982).

Gaiduk, I. *The Soviet Union and the Vietnam War* (Chicago: Ivan R. Dee, 1996).

Gardner, L. *Approaching Vietnam: From World War II through Dienbienphu* (New York: Norton, 1988).

Gardner, L. *Pay Any Price: Lyndon Johnson and the Wars for Vietnam* (Chicago: Ivan R. Dee, 1995).

Gelb, L. & Betts, R. *The Irony of Vietnam: The System Worked* (Washington: Brookings Institution, 1979).

Gettleman, M. *et al. Vietnam and America: The Most Comprehensive Documented History of the Vietnam War* (New York: Grove Press, 1995).

Haldeman, H. *The Ends of Power* (New York: Times Books, 1978).

Herring, G. *America's Longest War: the United States and Vietnam, 1950–1975* (New York: McGraw-Hill, 1986).

Herring, G. *LBJ and Vietnam: A Different Kind of War* (Austin: University of Texas Press, 1994).

Hess, G. *Vietnam and the United States: Origins and Legacy of War* (Boston: Twayne, 1990).

Hess, G. 'The unending debate: Historians and the Vietnam War', *Diplomatic History*, 18/2, 1994.

Ho Chi Minh *Selected Writings, 1920–1969* (Hanoi: Foreign Languages Publishing House, 1973).

Hoan Van Hoan *A Drop in the Ocean: Hoan Van Hoan's Revolutionary Reminiscences* (Beijing: Foreign Languages Publishing House, 1988).

Horne, A. *A Savage War of Peace: Algeria 1954–1962* (London, 1978).

Hunt, M. *Lyndon Johnson's War: America's Cold War Crusade in Vietnam, 1945–1965* (New York: Hill & Wang, 1996).

Isaacs, A. *Without Honor: Defeat in Vietnam and Cambodia*, (Baltimore: Johns Hopkins University, 1983).

Johnson, L. *The Vantage Point: Perspectives of the Presidency, 1963–69* (New York: Holt, Rinehart & Winston, 1971).

Kahin, G. *Intervention: How America Became Involved in Vietnam* (New York: Doubleday, 1986).

Karnow, S. *Vietnam: A History* (London: Century Hutchinson, 1983).

Kearns, D. *Lyndon Johnson and the American Dream* (New York: Harper & Row, 1976).

Kimball, J. (ed.) *To Reason Why: The Debate about the Causes of US Involvement in the Vietnam War* (New York: McGraw-Hill, 1990).

Kissinger, H. *The White House Years* (Boston: Little Brown, 1979).

Kolko, G. *Anatomy of a War: Vietnam, the United States, and the Modern Historical Experience* (New York: The New Press, 1994).

Lacouture, J. *Ho Chi Minh* (London: Allen Lane, 1968).

LaFeber, W. 'Roosevelt, Churchill, and Indochina, 1942–45', *American Historical Review*, Vol. 80 (1975).

LaFeber, W. *America, Russia and the Cold War 1945–1992* (New York: McGraw-Hill, 7th edn, 1993).

Levy, D. *The Debate over Vietnam* (Baltimore: Johns Hopkins University Press, 1991).

Lewy, G. *America in Vietnam* (New York: Oxford University Press, 1978).

Lomperis, T. *The War Everyone Lost – And Won: America's Intervention in Vietnam's Twin Struggles* (Baton Rouge, Louisiana: Louisiana State University, 1984).

McMahon, R. (ed.) *Major Problems in the History of the Vietnam War: Documents and Essays* (Lexington, Massachusetts: Heath & Co., 1995).

McNamara, R. *In Retrospect: The Tragedy and Lessons of Vietnam* (New York: Random House, 1995).

Maclear, M. *The Ten Thousand Day War: Vietnam, 1945–1975* (New York: St. Martin's Press, 1981).

New York Times 'Johnson, in 1964, saw war in Vietnam as pointless' (15 February 1997).

Newman, J. *JFK and Vietnam: Deception, Intrigue, and the Struggle for Power* (New York: Praeger, 1989).

Qiang Zhai 'China and the Geneva Conference of 1954', *The China Quarterly,* Vol. 129, 1992.

Qiang Zhai 'Transplanting the Chinese Model: Chinese Military Advisers and the first Vietnam War, 1950–1954', *Journal of Military History,* Vol. 57, 1993a.

Qiang Zhai 'China and the First Indochina War', *The China Quarterly,* Vol. 133, 1993b.

Qiang Zhai 'Beijing and the Vietnam Conflict, 1964–1965', *Cold War International History Bulletin,* Issue 6–7, 1995/6.

Race, J. *War Comes to Long An* (Berkeley: University of California Press, 1972).

Ruane, K. 'Containing America: Aspects of British Foreign Policy and the Cold War in Southeast Asia, 1951–54', *Diplomacy & Statecraft,* Vol. 7, 1996.

Short, A. *The Origins of the Vietnam War* (London: Longman, 1986).

Smith, R. *International History of the Vietnam War* (New York: St. Martin's Press, 3 volumes, 1983–90).

Stoessinger, J. *Crusaders and Pragmatists: Movers of Modern American Foreign Policy* (New York: Norton, 1979).

Summers, H. *On Strategy: A Critical Analysis of the Vietnam War* (New York, 1984).

Thayer, C. *War by Other Means: National Liberation and Revolution in Viet-Nam, 1954–1960* (Cambridge, Massachusetts: Unwin Hyman, 1989).

Truong Nhu Tang *A Vietcong Memoir* (New York: Harcourt Brace Jovanovich, 1986).

Turley, W. *The Second Indochina War: A Short Military and Political History* (Boulder, Colorado: Westview, 1986).

US Defense Department *The Pentagon Papers, Senator Gravel Edition;*

The Defense Department History of United States Decisionmaking on Vietnam (4 volumes, Boston: Beacon Press, 1971 onwards).

US State Department *Foreign Relations of the United States* [FRUS] (US Government Printing Office, Washington DC, various volumes on Vietnam and Southeast Asia, 1970s onwards).

Vandemark, B. *Into the Quagmire: Lyndon Johnson and the Escalation of the Vietnam War* (Oxford: Oxford University Press, 1991).

Werner, J. & Luu Doan Huynh (eds) *The Vietnam War: Vietnamese and American Perspectives* (New York: M.E. Sharpe, 1993).

Wintle, J. *The Viet Nam Wars* (London: Weidenfeld & Nicolson, 1991).

Young, M. *The Vietnam Wars, 1945–1990* (New York: Harper-Perrenial, 1991).

Young, M. 'The closest of hindsight' *Diplomatic History*, 20/3, 1996.

Index